BOOKS BY DANIEL J. BOORSTIN

Democracy and Its Discontents

* * *

The Americans: The Colonial Experience

The Americans: The National Experience

The Americans: The Democratic Experience

* * *

The Mysterious Science of the Law

The Lost World of Thomas Jefferson

The Genius of American Politics

America and the Image of Europe

The Image: A Guide to Pseudo-Events in America

The Decline of Radicalism

The Sociology of the Absurd

The Chicago History of

American Civilization (27 vols.; editor)

An American Primer (editor)

American Civilization (editor)

* * *

for young readers

The Landmark History of the American People

Vol. I: From Plymouth to Appomattox

Vol. II: From Appomattox to the Moon

☆ ☆ ☆

DEMOCRACY AND ITS DISCONTENTS

REFLECTIONS ON EVERYDAY AMERICA

DEMOCRACY AND ITS DISCONTENTS

☆ ☆ ☆ ☆ ☆ ☆ ☆

REFLECTIONS ON EVERYDAY AMERICA

DANIEL J. BOORSTIN

RANDOM HOUSE NEW YORK

 Published in the United States by Random House, Inc., New York, and simultaneously in Canada by Random House of Canada Limited, Toronto.

Library of Congress Cataloging in Publication Data
Boorstin, Daniel Joseph, 1914-
Democracy and its discontents.

1. United States—Civilization—1945- —Addresses, essays, lectures. I. Title.
E169.02.B593 917.3'03'92 73-20571
ISBN 0-394-49146-7

Manufactured in the United States of America
3 5 7 9 8 6 4 2

To

CARL and MARY HUMELSINE

". . . love life, and so find the meaning of it."

"Content makes poor men rich;
discontent makes rich men poor."

—Benjamin Franklin

FOREWORD

There is an obvious cure for Failure—and that is Success. But what is the cure for Success? This is a characteristically American problem. Historians have often noted that revolutions are made not by the downtrodden but by the discontented. One reason for this is that for the miseries of the poor, the deprived, and the oppressed there are well-known cures. With food we can cure starvation. But the malaise of the well-off, the sense of surfeit of the overfed, the resentment of those who have begun to receive their due but feel (however rightfully) that they have not yet got quite enough, the bewilderment of those who have been stirred to feel "needs" that they don't really feel until they are not sure whether or not their real needs are being satisfied—what are we to do for these? Can we be surprised, then, that our characteristic national ailments are not misery, deprivation, or oppression, but malaise, resentment, and bewilderment?

This book is not, in the main, about our miseries. It is not about poverty, disease, war, or the denial of essential human rights—although, of course, our nation has known, and still knows, all these. The flagrant violations of man's humanity are everybody's target. This book is not about crime, corruption, or the abuses of political or economic power that make the headlines. Our country has not lacked its eloquent voices, its organizers and leaders and spokesmen for the American conscience.

This book is not so much about our conscience as about our consciousness. Here I am not concerned with our sins and our crimes, but with our irritations and everyday frustrations, with some of the ways we feel unfulfilled, with our excess of some everyday resources, and with our failures to draw on or to create others. Here I am less concerned with how to build a Good Life or a Good Society than with how each of us feels about the prospects of each day.

I try in these chapters to describe some of the daily costs of some of our more remarkable successes. When before has a citizenry been offered so much news, so much up-to-the-minute information about itself and the whole world, so many and such prompt and such vivid images of current events? When before have people been offered so multitudinous and so rapidly changing an array of things and services, or had thrust on them so many interesting and ingenious promises of relief from the minor discomforts of life, promises of new delights in daily experience? When before have people been given so many everyday reasons for believing the past to be old-fashioned and obsolete? American civilization seems to thrive not merely on the planned obsolescence of last year's products and services, but on the planned obsolescence of the whole past. When before was there so widespread, so flourishing, so thorough a Democracy of Things?

In the first part of this book I describe the new flood of information which comes to late-twentieth-century Americans. Information about anything and everything, instant information about our own opinions and everybody else's opinions (or lack of opinions). In the second part I describe how this flood of information, and how the opportunities to tear down the old and replace it with the new, have limited our vistas. What does the omnipresent present do to our capacity to use the past? And finally, in the third part, I describe some of the peculiarities of American ideals, and how the kinds of fulfillment our nation has set itself affect the kinds of fulfillment that each of us can (or cannot) find. And I end by describing our characteristically American need for constant renewal.

While I try to remind us of some of the everyday costs of American civilization in our time, I am obviously not trying in this volume to offer an inventory or survey of American democracy, or to cast up the whole account. I have made an effort at such a survey in *The Americans: The Democratic Experience* (Random House, 1973).

Readers will find that I bring both good news and bad. For while I suggest that some of the most troublesome ills of our daily lives are minor, I also suggest that they may be incurable. They may be the inevitable price of achievements. We have been raised in the boosterish belief that if

American Democracy is good, it must be without cost. But such a view has not been shared by our wisest statesmen, moralists, and philosophers, from William Bradford, John Winthrop, Benjamin Franklin, Thomas Jefferson, and John Adams, through Abraham Lincoln and William James. They have thought that while American civilization (like all other human enterprises) would not be cost-free, America would offer men and women the resources, the knowledge, and the freedom to cast up the accounts for themselves, and so not be condemned to accept blindly the legacy of the past or the patronage of their rulers.

It has commonly been remarked that the early New England Puritans could not be disillusioned, for the simple reason that they never suffered from illusions. In this volume it is not my purpose to dispraise American Democracy—one of man's most amazing and surprising achievements on this earth—but rather to help prevent us from being disillusioned. That we can accomplish only if we make an honest, ruthless effort to see the price tag that history has placed on our civilization.

* * *

This book is a revision of the William W. Cook Lectures on American Institutions which I delivered at the University of Michigan, in Ann Arbor, April 3–7, 1972. Those lectures provided the incentive and the occasion to bring together some reflections on American democracy which arise from the peculiar circumstances of the latter part of the twentieth century. The following chapters are a substantial reshaping of the lectures. Several chapters have come out of later reflections stirred by those lectures and the discussions which followed them. And I have included other reflections, some dating from before the lectures, and others arising since, which have seemed helpful to give coherence to the subjects first explored at Ann Arbor. The book as a whole does, I hope, retain some of the informality of the spoken word. And, I hope, it may in some measure justify the purposes of the William W. Cook Lectureship and support its tradition of focusing our concern on the vitality of our institutions.

CONTENTS

THREE

ONE

☆ ☆

I

OVERCOMMUNICATION: ☆ ARE WE TALKING TOO MUCH? ☆

We suffer from a disease different from that which any society before us has suffered. I call it "overcommunication." I hesitate even to write about it because, by adding to the daily torrent of words, I aggravate the disease.

Yet, at the same time, as the prophetic humorist Tom Lehrer observes in one of his songs, it seems that nowadays everyone is complaining that he can't communicate. Parents complain that they can't communicate with children, children that they can't communicate with parents, students that they can't communicate with teachers, teachers that they can't communicate with students. And Lehrer wisely concludes that if a person cannot communicate, the least he ought to be able to do is to shut up.

We might begin to solve our problem of communication

if more of us took his advice. And we can better understand his good sense if we look briefly at the history of the idea of communication.

"Communicate" is a very old word which has had many meanings in the course of its history. One of the earliest, giving us some of its forgotten flavor, dates back to Starkey's *History of England* in 1538, where the word "communicate" is part of the definition of God. Starkey says that God is He who "communicated" His goodness to all others. This, of course, is related to the word "communicant," a person who shares in the Eucharist. So, in origin, "communicate" is related to the word "common," or "community," and it means somehow to make common, to share.

In one sense we could actually define the rise of civilization as the rise of communication—the improvement of the ways of sharing and the improvement of that which is shared. It is obvious that the quality of any civilization will depend on what there is to share and on how it is shared. And democracy, more than any other form of government, is based on the faith that sharing the good things of life—and especially sharing the power to govern—can be wholesome.

But in our enthusiasm for sharing and in our current mania for *more* communication, we have tended to forget the original and primary sense of the word, and unfortunately, to emphasize a secondary sense of "communicate." In this secondary sense, "communicate" (our dictionaries say) means "to impart information, knowledge or the like, to impart or convey knowledge of or inform a person of, to tell." Even this sense begins to be lost as its indispensable counterpart, the right to listen—or not to listen—begins to disappear.

While the progress of civilization is an improvement in what we share and in the processes of sharing, there is another commonly forgotten essential to the rise of civilization. As Sigmund Freud reminds us, an indispensable feature of civilization is the willingness of people *not* to say and *not* to do many things they might want to say or do. From this point of view, then, civilization consists just as much in how men do *not* communicate with others. In fact, this is one way of describing a decent society and in its most everyday form a way of describing good manners.

Good manners consist not only in our willingness to say what we *are* expected to say, but just as much in our self-control in keeping ourselves from saying what we really feel and really want to say, but which might hurt others. When someone says, "How are you today?" we say, "Fine, thanks, and how are you?" It's not good manners to go into the details of our sleeplessness last night, and how those pills didn't manage to conquer our insomnia, and so on. When we've been to a party and we leave it, we tell our host, "Thanks for a very nice evening." We don't usually say how boring it was, that we wish there had been some interesting people there, and that we had expected better refreshments. There was once a professor of ethics at Harvard who made it a practice to tell his hosts exactly what he felt at the end of a Cambridge evening. People said they found his lack of inhibition amusing, but they stopped inviting him to their parties.

Not only good manners are at stake here. For the very progress of civilization depends on the ability of people to develop a more self-controlled attitude about what they say —and how, when, and where. Human progress is the movement from expression to communication, from the growl, the snort, or the expletive to the mathematical formula or the narrative sentence. It is marked by the decline of the exclamation point.

The rise of exposition, of abstraction, and of "communication" marks a vast increase in the range of *what* can be communicated, and a widening in the geographic and chronological range of those *to whom* it can be communicated. At the same time it marks a movement from the yelp of pain or the scream of rage to sounds and symbols that may be of greater interest and deeper meaning to people in other times and other places.

This means, too, a shift of focus from the self, from the simple expression of emotions in gesture and voice, to the carrying of messages of facts and ideas, even of feelings. In modern times, and especially in a democratic society, decency and progress depend on the willingness of people to forgo whatever sense of release or catharsis might come from the screamed expletive or the personal yelp, in favor of other forms of sounds and symbols.

Representative institutions, of all institutions, depend most on the willingness of people to inhibit their animal emotions and to talk to others with respect. In countries like France and Italy, where representative assemblies have been marked by the throwing of inkwells, the shouting of libels and curses, and the punching of noses, representative government is fragile and erratic. And in those like Great Britain, where the representative assembly has been marked by a certain inhibition, a certain ritual, and a formalized way of showing respect for other members, representative government is more stable and more effective.

Until now, the representative institutions of our country have, fortunately, fallen in the latter category—of the etiquette-inhibited, ritualized parliamentary bodies. Anyone who comes to Washington from a college campus cannot fail to be cheered by the frequent expressions of respect by legislators for other legislators with whom they disagree.

Our democracy then, in Jefferson's familiar but neglected phrase, rests on a "decent respect to the opinions of mankind."

The Declaration of Independence was motivated by, among other things, American feelings of anger and outrage against King George III and the members of his government. Yet it did not attack the king as an idiot or lunatic. Nor did it scream curses or identify the king with unsavory or unmentionable physical or sexual acts. It did not even accuse George III or his government of corruption and incompetence, which it might very well have done. The declaration simply declared some rights and some grievances in measured, even legalistic language. If the Declaration of Independence had been a volcano of expletives, it would have had little effect in its day and would have been buried with other sub-literature long before our time. Much of our daily problem of communication arises from our unwillingness to show a similar decency and self-restraint.

Perhaps the most important single change in the human consciousness in the last century, and especially in the American consciousness, has been the multiplying of the means and forms of what we call "communication." Not so long ago, a person had to make a special effort to get a message in from the world around him. For news he had to purchase a newspaper. For other information or entertainment, he had to buy a book or attend a lecture, which was expensive, or find a traveler, who might be scarce, or go to a theater, which performed only occasionally.

Nowadays communication is an everywhere all-the-time thing. To escape messages we have to make a special effort —and we seldom succeed. Even when we come into our own living room we cannot avoid a glimpse of some far-off stage on the television screen being watched by someone else in the family. New forms of involuntary reception— from telephone solicitations to the sound of music in elevators to the loudspeaker witticisms of an airplane captain —remind us that there's always somebody out there trying to tell us something—in fact, demanding to tell us something—and there is no escape.

We have become so accustomed to all this that we begin to feel lonesome or even neglected and wonder whether we are really alive and alert when we do not hear these sounds. People travel miles to walk on deserted beaches or mountainsides—then try to keep in touch by carrying a transistor radio. I find myself listening to the radio not only in my automobile as I drive to work but even in my shower.

Along with the "everywhereness" and multiplication of messages comes repetition. Every hour on the hour, sometimes on the quarter-hour, all the news, all the time. And when there's no news there's an interview or a "special report." People grow calluses in their ears. It actually becomes harder and harder to get a message through. We witness the cheapening of the word. Wherever we go and wherever we look, we see and hear words—mostly messages we would rather not receive. Once, the word was sacred, a synonym for the Word of God, that which has a special sanctity. But now, words are everywhere and inescapable.

There is no better clue to the decline of the original sense of "communication" than the decline of prayer—not only in the schoolroom but everywhere else. Prayer is a form of communication, a form of sharing. And one of its more eloquent forms is silence. But silence itself has become so rare that it seems unnatural, and even terrifying. Silent prayer is not at all congenial to our age.

A society like ours, which puts so much of its resources into communication, inevitably overvalues communication. We begin to lose our sense of its proper values and proper boundaries. We begin to lose our sense of the difference between communication and expression. We begin to expect the impossible from the mere act of communication. We meet in conventions where people are expected to produce wisdom or knowledge out of their pooled ignorance or prejudices. We meet in committees, conferences, and discussion groups without knowing our purpose and then adjourn without knowing whether we have accomplished it.

In our world of callused ears and overtaxed eyes, there are many symptoms of the desperate need of people to make somebody listen, to be sure somehow that somebody is hearing. More and more people are willing to pay fees they cannot afford, to medically trained psychiatric listeners who listen, nod, and take notes. A few desperate people, especially young people with great energy who find they cannot get people to listen when they say something, decide instead to *throw* something.

No society could survive—and surely no society could be decent—if everybody in it were able to communicate everything. Democracy thrives on selective communication. And to keep the society democratic, the selection must be made not by some outside political agency, but by the self-controlled citizen.

With the rise of photography and the movies, of radio and television, and with the improvement and diffusion of the graphic arts, an ever-larger proportion of what is communicated becomes vivid. To catch and hold our attention, the images must be in motion. So it is not surprising that more and more of what is communicated to us is explosive and disruptive, interrupting the current of our experience.

There is a natural tendency, then, to identify communication with dissent, with the violent and the melodramatic. This has the retrograde—we might more precisely call it "reactionary"—effect of leading us backward to identify communication with expression, with saying what *I* feel rather than what may have meaning to you. And so, inevitably, we tend to identify communication with that which emphasizes the separateness of each individual.

But democracy depends on the communication which is sharing, not on that which is purely self-expressive, explosive, or vituperative. Our new opportunities and our new temptations to overcommunicate require a new and harder self-discipline among citizens, one of the most difficult forms of discipline to enforce. It illustrates the wisdom of the English judge who said, "Civilization must be measured by the extent of obedience to the unenforceable." In a world of overcommunication, the survival of a decent society may depend on our willingness to accept this truth.

We show respect for ourselves and for our fellow-men and we affirm our belief that there may be something larger and even less intelligible than ourselves by admitting that not everything can or should be said. In this nation, which has spent more of its resources than any other to produce a wise and educated citizenry, we must not forget the commonplace wisdom of an old Japanese proverb: "He who knows nothing else knows enough if he knows when to be silent."

II

☆ HOW OPINION WENT PUBLIC ☆

Just as the decline of monarchy can be traced in the declining reputation of aristocracies, so, too, the rise of democracy is the story of the rising reputation of "Opinion." Something that was at first personal (thought to be unreliable, and even slightly disreputable) grew into a vast and dominant public institution. "Opinion" has had a startling career. Though the materials for that story are handy, the story is seldom recounted. Just as it was uncommon (and even considered dangerous) in earlier times to scrutinize the origins of the supposed virtues of the ruling aristocracy, so nowadays we take for granted the pedigree and credentials of our ruling-power, which is Public Opinion.

This rise of opinion is one of the more striking success stories in the history of ideas. "Opinion" is the name for a belief or conclusion held with confidence but not necessarily substantiated by positive knowledge or proof. Opinions, then, are distinguished by the strength with which they are held rather than by the authenticity with which their conclusions are demonstrable. According to the *Oxford English Dictionary,* the primary sense of the word is: "What one thinks or how one thinks about something; judgement resting on grounds insufficient for complete demonstration; belief of something as probable, or as seeming to one's own mind to be true, though not certain or established. (Distinguished from *knowledge, conviction,* or *certainty*; but sometimes = belief)." The word and the idea have an interesting career in which there are three stages.

In the beginning, "opinion" was a synonym for uncertainty—for a notion grounded in personal preference (rather than fact), and hence was thought likely to be the pathway to error. The earliest use of the word in print seems to go back to 1388, when Thomas Usk, a Lord Mayor of London who was executed, presumably for his dangerous political opinions, observed, "Opinion is while a thing is in non certaine, & hidde frome mens very knowledging, and by no parfite reason fully declared." "Nothing is so easily cheated, nor so commonly mistaken," Sir William Temple remarked in the late seventeenth century, "as vulgar Opinion." Until the rise and triumph of liberalism in Europe, "opinion" was closely identified with error, and to say that something was "mere opinion" was a way of saying the notion was hardly worth taking account of.

Then, by the late eighteenth century, when representative government, Protestantism, and modern liberalism had taken firm root in Western Europe, "Opinion" acquired different overtones. Now, "Opinion" was frequently qualified by such words as *common, general,* or *public,* and emphasis shifted from its uncertainty or error-prone quality to something else—to its power. Here was a hint, too—in the age of the Baron de Montesquieu, David Hume, Adam Smith, and Edward Gibbon—a hint of the rise of the new social sciences, which were less intent on moralizing than on describing the forces at work in society. Gibbon, for example, in his *Decline and Fall of the Roman Empire,* traced the currents of public opinion as forces in ancient history. In that descriptive age, writers began to characterize this force as if it were something newly discovered and perhaps only recently created. Accordingly, Christof Wieland, the German man of letters, in 1798 wrote that public opinion was

> an opinion that gradually takes root among a whole people; especially among those who have the most influence when they work together as a group. In this way it wins the upper hand to such an extent that one meets it everywhere. It is an opinion that without being noticed takes possession of most heads, and even in situations where it does not dare express itself out loud it can be recognized by a louder and louder muffled murmur. It then only requires some small opening that will allow it air, and it will break out with force. Then it can change whole nations in a brief time and give whole parts of the world a new configuration.

As representative institutions came to dominate several countries in Western Europe, and as democracy came to the United States, Opinion (only so recently recognized as powerful) actually became reputable. And it was not long before men of letters and public figures (just as they had been tempted to sycophancy of the monarch and of powerful noblemen) were lavishing praise on Opinion (now widely known as "Public Opinion"). In 1801 Thomas Jefferson referred gratefully to "the mighty wave of public opinion which has rolled over our republic" and which had brought him to the Presidency. Since then, only a few American politicians, and almost none who survive to be noticed by a later generation, have dared not to praise the wisdom of Public Opinion. Most have gone out of their way to puff the virtues of their master. Franklin Delano Roosevelt, one of our most popular and most effective Presidents, also was one of the most eloquent and most consistent in his praise of Public Opinion. "The average opinion of mankind," he observed in what became a commonplace, "is in the long run superior to the dictates of the self-chosen."

Now we are usually told that the great advance of democracy gave people a right to express themselves, and that the decline of monarchy and of aristocracy signaled the Decline of Authority—while the rise of democracy announced the Rise of Reason. There is a good deal of truth in both these historical clichés.

But they neglect one dramatic episode in the rise of Opinion: how Opinion went Public. The rise of Opinion, as the three stages of its meaning indicate, had been a product of new ways of gathering numerous individual preferences (rational or irrational) into a much more potent single collective judgment. Private opinions somehow have been collected and congealed into Public Opinion. After the triumph of representative government, the representatives needed to be responsive to the people. If they wanted to stay in office they had to know, and if possible to anticipate, the wishes of the voters. Democracy obviously meant a new opportunity for citizens to express their preferences and to be heard by those who ruled them.

It meant something else, too: a new opportunity for citizens to learn the preferences of *other* citizens. The ballot box for the first time gave each citizen the opportunity to know *other people's opinions.* It made superfluous much of the earlier subterranean apparatus of the people who wanted to change their governments, and who were forced secretly, and sometimes illegally, to seek out the extent and the identity of dissidents. Where the ballot box was honest and the suffrage was wide, it made revolution both more easy and less necessary. And then people could say with the English poet-laureate-pundit, Alfred Austin, in 1887:

> Public opinion is no more than this;
> What people think that other people think.

Opinion was well on the way to going public. The ballot box was only the crucial first stage in the modern democratic process of congealing private opinions into Public Opinion, a vast mysterious new power. Government-sponsored elections revealed to each citizen the opinions of other citizens on the candidates for public office, and on public policies. Then came the rise of a democratized economy, and the improved machinery for bringing everything to everybody. Mass democracy brought mass production, and mass marketing made it necessary for manufacturers, advertisers, retailers, and others to know the preferences of everybody about everything. And out of the needs of mass marketing and mass advertising, there grew the Opinion Polls. Before long, the techniques of modern opinion polling (which used sophisticated scientific sampling) were applied to politics and used by journalists and by candidates, congressmen, and political parties. By the late twentieth century there appeared to be a discoverable "Public Opinion" (measurable to fractions of percentages) on nearly every public or private question, and on any product, service, or person of possible interest to any man, woman, or child. Americans became accustomed to learning of these Public Opinions every day in the newspapers, on radio, on television, in printed or spoken advertisements or TV commercials.

When Opinion went public, there was a crucial change in the prestige of all opinions. An individual's opinion, naturally enough, seemed flimsy and unreliable. For it had all the fallibility of that particular person, and was obviously tainted by that person's ignorance or prejudice. "Public" Opinion, however, had quite a different character. Being the opinion of nobody in particular, but of everybody in general, its weaknesses were hard to define and its strength was enveloped in an aura of group wisdom. Did it not include the reasoned conclusions of the learned along with the commonsense intuitions of the untutored? Might it not hold the best of all realms of thought or feeling?

Public Opinion seemed as much more respectable than Private Opinion as the force of an army seemed more respectable than the force of an armed individual. Even the most critical observers began to think that Public Opinion was worthy of the power it commanded. As Lord Bryce remarked in 1921:

> Public opinion, that is the mind and conscience of a whole nation, is the opinion of persons who are included in the parties; for the parties taken together are the nation. Yet it [public opinion] stands above the parties being cooler and larger-minded than they are. It is the product of a greater number of minds than in any other country, and it is indisputably sovereign. It is the central point in the whole American polity.

By the late twentieth century there had come into being in the United States something which I will call "Big Opinion." Just as large-scale organization, concentration of capital, and new technologies brought into being "Big Science," so it was with the machinery of making, forming, shaping, testing, assessing, and organizing opinion. A whole new technology of polling and sampling became the basis of a prosperous industry. Opinion pollsters formed themselves into professional societies, they produced learned journals, and trade journals. At the same time the new professions of advertising and public relations (drawing every day on the products of this new industry) enlisted some of the best-educated, brightest, and most sophisticated minds in the nation. When opinion measuring and opinion making had become big business, the power and prestige of Public Opinion reached a new stage.

What are the characteristics of the individual opinions which make up this Big Opinion? Without entering the quagmires of epistemology, we can list a few of these characteristics, which also offer us clues to the special discontents of democracy in our time.

1. *Opinions are miscellaneous, discrete, and unsystematic.* While elements of knowledge are somehow coherent and have a necessary relationship to one another, opinions are discrete and may be contradictory. A person may have two opinions which actually contradict each other, yet he finds that both are his opinions, strongly held.

2. *Opinions tend to be normative:* approve or disapprove, yes or no, good or bad. Knowledge tends to start from a question (How? When? Where? What?), so knowledge concerns What's What, but opinions concern So What? Opinions tend to start from an answer to a question: What is your conclusion about him or her, this or that?

3. *Opinions, therefore, tend to be fluctuating and fluid, not cumulative.* Knowledge builds on knowledge. But one opinion may or may not add on to another. While knowledge grows, opinions oscillate.

4. *Opinions can be about the future,* while knowledge can only be about the past. (Or the present, a name for the immediate past.) Therefore,

5. *Opinions are limitless in subject,* infinite in number. They may be about anything that exists—or about people, things, and subjects which do not exist.

6. *Opinions are validated by other opinions.* Of course, no amount of agreement can create a fact of life or transform assertion into fact. While majority vote cannot create knowledge, it can create opinion: one person's opinion can become stronger and be reinforced because it is also held by others.

7. Finally, and perhaps more important, *Opinions tend to be epiphenomenal.* While knowledge tends to be phenomenal, concerning facts that are directly perceptible to the senses, opinions tend to be derivative and secondary. While knowledge is *of* this or that, opinions are *about* this or that.

In a functioning democracy, a responsible citizen is one who has opinions and expresses them. In the United States we tend to talk not about the wise, the knowledgeable, or the prudent citizen, but rather about the "well-informed" citizen. It is important, we are commonly told, that our citizenry be "well informed." Our newspapers, our radio programs, and our television are all crucial to our institutions because they keep citizens "well informed."

"Information," then, is the essential thing—the material from which the "informed" citizen is expected to shape his opinion. And what characterizes "information" by contrast with other data about the world? Its most prominent and distinctive characteristic is its randomness. Knowledge is a coherent structure, where each part is related to every other, and where discovery consists of finding these relationships. (William James defined a genius as a person especially adept in this ability.) But any scrap of data is information. And in our time the most characteristic form of information is news. For, by definition, news consists of new bits of information. One piece of news need have no clear relationship to any other bit of news. And that very staccato, miscellaneous character is part of the newspaper's charm and appeal. It can be the fact that Muskogee, Oklahoma, experienced its heaviest rainfall in twenty years, or that automobile mechanics in Teheran have gone on strike, or that a well-known movie star is planning a divorce, or that a new kind of hairbrush is on the market. It is no wonder that in a democracy, where every citizen is expected to have an opinion on anything and everything, the characteristic form of data is information, and the dominant form of information is news.

Nor is it surprising that, in the guise of informing us, the merchandisers of information flood us with unlimited quantities of fact, statistics, rumor, or speculation. Is there any limit to what might help a conscientious citizen form opinions about the past, present, or future? Who can tell precisely what information will help us form countless opinions about subjects still to be discovered, and persons yet unknown. Again, with characteristic American optimism, we assume that too-much is always better than not-enough. Is it not impossible that any citizen could be *over*informed? And so it is that with abundant news (every hour on the hour, on the half-hour, and in between) and good intentions, we pave the road to Overcommunication.

III

TV MYOPIA: ☆ TOO MUCH ☆ TOO SOON

Television has conquered the nation with blitzkrieg speed and has received unconditional surrender. A bewildered America still hasn't found its bearings. For television has brought us Too Much Too Soon. Without anybody having planned it so, we feel our heads swimming with instant experience. We get our news before anybody (including the commentator) has had a chance to reflect on what it means or whether it's worth being called news. If our TV myopia is not to become an incurable history-blindness, an inability to see beyond this evening's screen, we must find antidotes for Too Much Too Soon.

We Americans have been a racing-people—anxious to get there first with anything and everything. And we have worried less about where we were going or why than about how we could get wherever-it-is with whatever-it-may-be before anybody else. This mania has goaded and inspired and troubled us as individuals and as a nation. It has populated our continent and built our cities and suburbs, has led us to go underground and deep into mountains for gold and silver and oil and uranium, has spread new products across the country, and now leads us out to the moon and to other planets. Our appetite for Getting There First has helped us to greatness as a nation, but it also tempts us into national habits which threaten to pull us apart.

An everyday example is the desperate quest for TV programs that are "relevant." But what people call "relevance" is not really that at all. What they are talking about most of the time is not the relevant but the topical.

Topical (from the Greek word *topos* for "place") means that which is special to some particular place or time. "Topics of the Day" are the events which, having just happened, are peculiar to that day. We like to read or hear about them because they remind us that we are alive, that there is something special to our lifetime. The topical reinforces our mood with an exclamation point, but does not enlarge or illuminate. Hear this! See that! That's what we say when we point to something topical. On TV, characteristic statements of the topical are the video-taped clips of the day's events offered staccato on the news. The topical event—an earthquake, an airplane hijacking, a hotel fire, or an assassination—is announced and diffused but seldom explained at the time.

The *relevant* is something quite different. "Relevant" comes from the Latin *relevans*, which means lifting or raising. To show the relevance of something is to lift it above the current of daily topics, to connect it with distant events and larger issues. The search for relevance is a search for connections that don't at first meet the eye, that will be just as valid—and even more interesting—tomorrow and the day after.

A topical fact becomes every moment less newsworthy. But a historical event is always growing in historical significance. The American Revolution became more interesting after the French Revolution, and both became still more so after the Russian Revolution and after the Chinese Revolution, and after President Nixon's visit to Communist China.

The search for topical items overwhelms us with opinions. For nearly everybody has instant opinions on nearly everything—from mothers-in-law to group sex to cigarette smoking to inflation and Vietnam. The popular talk shows provide opinions which are supposed to be all the more interesting because they are expressed by people just as ignorant as you and I. Opinions, too, are pre-eminently topical. They shift with the latest news, with the company a person keeps, and with the state of his digestion. Knowledge (another name for what is relevant and stays relevant), on the other hand, doesn't change with the mood or with the cleverness of the questioner or the attitudes of others on the panel. But somehow there doesn't seem to be enough knowledge to go around.

Perhaps the essential problem (for which there may be no solution in a free and well-to-do nation) is that we have too many TV stations broadcasting too many hours. In their desperate effort to fill thousands of hours weekly, they are understandably tempted to give us more "information" than there really is. But even so, there is much that can be done today to shift TV offerings from the topical to the relevant. What we need are fewer talk shows, fewer interviews, fewer odd-ball quizzes, fewer celebrity say-sos.

And fewer newscasts. We need programs that bring us less of the "up-to-the-minute" stuff, which every passing minute makes obsolete, and more knowledge. Fewer "situation comedies" and situation tragedies, but more comedy and more tragedy. Fewer reports of today's catastrophe and fewer clichés of today's "burning issues," but deeper visual documentation.

In a word, what we need are more programs about something, and fewer programs about everything. More programs about how something really happened, how the world has changed and is changing. More about people who do things and make things, about how they're done and made, and less about people who say the kooky and do the ridiculous. TV will then be less a solvent and more a cement in our American community.

IV

THE RHETORIC OF DEMOCRACY

Advertising, of course, has been part of the mainstream of American civilization, although you might not know it if you read the most respectable surveys of American history. It has been one of the enticements to the settlement of this New World, it has been a producer of the peopling of the United States, and in its modern form, in its world-wide reach, it has been one of our most characteristic products.

Never was there a more outrageous or more unscrupulous or more ill-informed advertising campaign than that by which the promoters for the American colonies brought settlers here. Brochures published in England in the seventeenth century, some even earlier, were full of hopeful overstatements, half-truths, and downright lies, along with some facts which nowadays surely would be the basis for a restraining order from the Federal Trade Commission. Gold and silver, fountains of youth, plenty of fish, venison without limit, all these were promised, and of course some of them were found. It would be interesting to speculate on how long it might have taken to settle this continent if there had not been such promotion by enterprising advertisers. How has American civilization been shaped by the fact that there was a kind of natural selection here of those people who were willing to believe advertising?

Advertising has taken the lead in promising and exploiting the new. This was a new world, and one of the advertisements for it appears on the dollar bill on the Great Seal of the United States, which reads *novus ordo seclorum*, one of the most effective advertising slogans to come out of this country. "A new order of the centuries"—belief in novelty and in the desirability of opening novelty to everybody has been important in our lives throughout our history and especially in this century. Again and again advertising has been an agency for inducing Americans to try anything and everything—from the continent itself to a new brand of soap. As one of the more literate and poetic of the advertising copywriters, James Kenneth Frazier, a Cornell graduate, wrote in 1900 in "The Doctor's Lament":

This lean M.D. is Dr. Brown
Who fares but ill in Spotless Town.
The town is so confounded clean,
It is no wonder he is lean,
He's lost all patients now, you know,
Because they use *Sapolio*.

The same literary talent that once was used to retail Sapolio was later used to induce people to try the Edsel or the Mustang, to experiment with Lifebuoy or Body-All, to drink Pepsi-Cola or Royal Crown Cola, or to shave with a Trac II razor.

And as expansion and novelty have become essential to our economy, advertising has played an ever-larger role: in the settling of the continent, in the expansion of the economy, and in the building of an American standard of living. Advertising has expressed the optimism, the hyperbole, and the sense of community, the sense of reaching which has been so important a feature of our civilization.

Here I wish to explore the significance of advertising, not as a force in the economy or in shaping an American standard of living, but rather as a touchstone of the ways in which we Americans have learned about all sorts of things.

The problems of advertising are of course not peculiar to advertising, for they are just one aspect of the problems of democracy. They reflect the rise of what I have called Consumption Communities and Statistical Communities, and many of the special problems of advertising have arisen from our continuously energetic effort to give everybody everything.

If we consider democracy not just as a political system, but as a set of institutions which do aim to make everything available to everybody, it would not be an overstatement to describe advertising as the characteristic rhetoric of democracy. One of the tendencies of democracy, which Plato and other antidemocrats warned against a long time ago, was the danger that rhetoric would displace or at least overshadow epistemology; that is, *the temptation to allow the problem of persuasion to overshadow the problem of knowledge.* Democratic societies tend to become more concerned with what people believe than with what is true, to become more concerned with credibility than with truth. All these problems become accentuated in a large-scale democracy like ours, which possesses all the apparatus of modern industry. And the problems are accentuated still further by universal literacy, by instantaneous communication, and by the daily plague of words and images.

In the early days it was common for advertising men to define advertisements as a kind of news. The best admen, like the best journalists, were supposed to be those who were able to make their news the most interesting and readable. This was natural enough, since the verb to "advertise" originally meant, intransitively, to take note or to consider. For a person to "advertise" meant originally, in the fourteenth and fifteenth centuries, to reflect on something, to think about something. Then it came to mean, transitively, to call the attention of another to something, to give him notice, to notify, admonish, warn or inform in a formal or impressive manner. And then, by the sixteenth century, it came to mean: to give notice of anything, to make generally known. It was not until the late eighteenth century that the word "advertising" in English came to have a specifically "advertising" connotation as we might say today, and not until the late nineteenth century that it began to have a specifically commercial connotation. By 1879 someone was saying, "Don't advertise unless you have something worth advertising." But even into the present century, newspapers continue to call themselves by the title "Advertiser"—for example, the Boston *Daily Advertiser*, which was a newspaper of long tradition and one of the most dignified papers in Boston until William Randolph Hearst took it over in 1917. Newspapers carried "Advertiser" on their mastheads, not because they sold advertisements but because they brought news.

Now, the main role of advertising in American civilization came increasingly to be that of persuading and appealing rather than that of educating and informing. By 1921, for instance, one of the more popular textbooks, Blanchard's *Essentials of Advertising*, began: "Anything employed to influence people favorably is advertising. The mission of advertising is to persuade men and women to act in a way that will be of advantage to the advertiser." This development—in a country where a shared, a rising, and a democratized standard of living was the national pride and the national hallmark—meant that advertising had become the rhetoric of democracy.

What, then, were some of the main features of modern American advertising—if we consider it as a form of rhetoric? First, and perhaps most obvious, is *repetition*. It is hard for us to realize that the use of repetition in advertising is not an ancient device but a modern one, which actually did not come into common use in American journalism until just past the middle of the nineteenth century.

The development of what came to be called "iteration copy" was a result of a struggle by a courageous man of letters and advertising pioneer, Robert Bonner, who bought the old New York *Merchant's Ledger* in 1851 and turned it into a popular journal. He then had the temerity to try to change the ways of James Gordon Bennett, who of course was one of the most successful of the American newspaper pioneers, and who was both a sensationalist and at the same time an extremely stuffy man when it came to things that he did not consider to be news. Bonner was determined to use advertisements in Bennett's wide-circulating New York *Herald* to sell his own literary product, but he found it difficult to persuade Bennett to allow him to use any but agate type in his advertising. (Agate was the smallest type used by newspapers in that day, only barely legible to the naked eye.) Bennett would not allow advertisers to use larger type, nor would he allow them to use illustrations except stock cuts, because he thought it was undignified. He said, too, that to allow a variation in the format of ads would be undemocratic. He insisted that all advertisers use the same size type so that no one would be allowed to prevail over another simply by presenting his message in a larger, more clever, or more attention-getting form.

Finally Bonner managed to overcome Bennett's rigidity by leasing whole pages of the paper and using the tiny agate type to form larger letters across the top of the page. In this way he produced a message such as "Bring home the New York Ledger tonight." His were unimaginative messages, and when repeated all across the page they technically did not violate Bennett's agate rule. But they opened a new era and presaged a new freedom for advertisers in their use of the newspaper page. Iteration copy—the practice of presenting prosaic content in ingenious, repetitive form—became common, and nowadays of course is commonplace.

. . .

A second characteristic of American advertising which is not unrelated to this is the development of *an advertising style*. We have histories of most other kinds of style—including the style of many unread writers who are remembered today only because they have been forgotten—but we have very few accounts of the history of advertising style, which of course is one of the most important forms of our language and one of the most widely influential.

The development of advertising style was the convergence of several very respectable American traditions. One of these was the tradition of the "plain style," which the Puritans made so much of and which accounts for so much of the strength of the Puritan literature. The "plain style" was of course much influenced by the Bible and found its way into the rhetoric of American writers and speakers of great power like Abraham Lincoln. When advertising began to be self-conscious in the early years of this century, the pioneers urged copywriters not to be too clever, and especially not to be fancy. One of the pioneers of the advertising copywriters, John Powers, said, for example, "The commonplace is the proper level for writing in business; where the first virtue is plainness, 'fine writing' is not only intellectual, it is offensive." George P. Rowell, another advertising pioneer, said, "You must write your advertisement to catch damned fools—not college professors." He was a very tactful person. And he added, "And you'll catch just as many college professors as you will of any other sort." In the 1920's, when advertising was beginning to come into its own, Claude Hopkins, whose name is known to all in the trade, said, "Brilliant writing has no place in advertising. A unique style takes attention from the subject. Any apparent effort to sell creates corresponding resistance. . . . One should be natural and simple. His language should not be conspicuous. In fishing for buyers, as in fishing for bass, one should not reveal the hook." So there developed a characteristic advertising style in which plainness, the phrase that anyone could understand, was a distinguishing mark.

At the same time, the American advertising style drew on another, and what might seem an antithetic, tradition—the tradition of hyperbole and tall talk, the language of Davy Crockett and Mike Fink. While advertising could think of itself as 99.44 percent pure, it used the language of "Toronado" and "Cutlass." As I listen to the radio in Washington, I hear a celebration of heroic qualities which would make the characteristics of Mike Fink and Davy Crockett pale, only to discover at the end of the paean that what I have been hearing is a description of the Ford dealers in the District of Columbia neighborhood. And along with the folk tradition of hyperbole and tall talk comes the rhythm of folk music. We hear that Pepsi-Cola hits the spot, that it's for the young generation—and we hear other products celebrated in music which we cannot forget and sometimes don't want to remember.

There grew somehow out of all these contradictory tendencies—combining the commonsense language of the "plain style," and the fantasy language of "tall talk"—an advertising style. This characteristic way of talking about things was especially designed to reach and catch the millions. It created a whole new world of myth. A myth, the dictionary tells us, is a notion based more on tradition or convenience than on facts; it is a received idea. Myth is not just fantasy and not just fact but exists in a limbo, in the world of the "Will to Believe," which William James has written about so eloquently and so perceptively. This is the world of the neither true nor false—of the statement that 60 percent of the physicians who expressed a choice said that our brand of aspirin would be more effective in curing a simple headache than any other leading brand.

That kind of statement exists in a penumbra. I would call this the "advertising penumbra." It is not untrue, and yet, in its connotation it is not exactly true.

Now, there is still another characteristic of advertising so obvious that we are inclined perhaps to overlook it. I call that *ubiquity*. Advertising abhors a vacuum and we discover new vacuums every day. The parable, of course, is the story of the man who thought of putting the advertisement on the other side of the cigarette package. Until then, that was wasted space and a society which aims at a democratic standard of living, at extending the benefits of consumption and all sorts of things and services to everybody, must miss no chances to reach people. The highway billboard and other outdoor advertising, bus and streetcar and subway advertising, and skywriting, radio and TV commercials—all these are of course obvious evidence that advertising abhors a vacuum.

We might reverse the old mousetrap slogan and say that anyone who can devise another place to put another mousetrap to catch a consumer will find people beating a path to his door. "Avoiding advertising will become a little harder next January," the *Wall Street Journal* reported on May 17, 1973, "when a Studio City, California, company launches a venture called StoreVision. Its product is a system of billboards that move on a track across supermarket ceilings. Some 650 supermarkets so far are set to have the system." All of which helps us understand the observation attributed to a French man of letters during his recent visit to Times Square. "What a beautiful place, if only one could not read!" Everywhere is a place to be filled, as we discover in a recent *Publishers Weekly* description of one advertising program: "The $1.95 paperback edition of Dr. Thomas A. Harris' million-copy best seller, 'I'm O.K., You're O.K.' is in for full-scale promotion in July by its publisher, Avon Books. Plans range from bumper stickers to airplane streamers, from planes flying above Fire Island, the Hamptons and Malibu. In addition, the $100,000 promotion budget calls for 200,000 bookmarks, plus brochures, buttons, lipcards, floor and counter displays, and advertising in magazines and TV."

The ubiquity of advertising is of course just another effect of our uninhibited efforts to use all the media to get all sorts of information to everybody everywhere. Since the places to be filled are everywhere, the amount of advertising is not determined by the *needs* of advertising, but by the *opportunities* for advertising which become unlimited.

But the most effective advertising, in an energetic, novelty-ridden society like ours, tends to be "self-liquidating." To create a cliché you must offer something which everybody accepts. The most successful advertising therefore self-destructs because it becomes cliché. Examples of this are found in the tendency for copyrighted names of trademarks to enter the vernacular—for the proper names of products which have been made familiar by costly advertising to become common nouns, and so to apply to anybody's products. Kodak becomes a synonym for camera, Kleenex a synonym for facial tissue, when both begin with a small *k*, and Xerox (now, too, with a small *x*) is used to describe all processes of copying, and so on. These are prototypes of the problem. If you are successful enough, then you will defeat your purpose in the long run—by making the name and the message so familiar that people won't notice them, and then people will cease to distinguish your product from everybody else's.

In a sense, of course, as we will see, the whole of American civilization is an example. When this was a "new" world, if people succeeded in building a civilization here, the New World would survive and would reach the time—in our age—when it would cease to be new. And now we have the oldest written Constitution in use in the world. This is only a parable of which there are many more examples.

The advertising man who is successful in marketing any particular product, then—in our high-technology, well-to-do democratic society, which aims to get everything to everybody—is apt to be diluting the demand for his particular product in the very act of satisfying it. But luckily for him, he is at the very same time creating a fresh demand for his services as advertiser.

And as a consequence, there is yet another role which is assigned to American advertising. This is what I call "erasure." Insofar as advertising is competitive or innovation is widespread, erasure is required in order to persuade consumers that this year's model is superior to last year's.

In fact, we consumers learn that we might be risking our lives if we go out on the highway with those very devices that were last year's lifesavers but without whatever special kind of brakes or wipers or seat belt is on this year's model. This is what I mean by "erasure"—and we see it on our advertising pages or our television screen every day. We read in the *New York Times* (May 20, 1973), for example, that "For the price of something small and ugly, you can drive something small and beautiful"—an advertisement for the Fiat 250 Spider. Or another, perhaps more subtle example is the advertisement for shirts under a picture of Oliver Drab: "Oliver Drab. A name to remember in fine designer shirts? No kidding. . . . Because you pay extra money for Oliver Drab. And for all the other superstars of the fashion world. Golden Vee [the name of the brand that is advertised] does not have a designer's label. But we do have designers. . . . By keeping their names *off* our label and simply saying Golden Vee, we can afford to sell our $7 to $12 shirts for just $7 to $12, which should make Golden Vee a name to remember. Golden Vee, you only pay for the shirt."

Having mentioned two special characteristics—the self-liquidating tendency and the need for erasure—which arise from the dynamism of the American economy, I would like to try to place advertising in a larger perspective. The special role of advertising in our life gives a clue to a pervasive oddity in American civilization. A leading feature of past cultures, as anthropologists have explained, is the tendency to distinguish between "high" culture and "low" culture—between the culture of the literate and the learned on the one hand and that of the populace on the other. In other words, between the language of literature and the language of the vernacular. Some of the most useful statements of this distinction have been made by social scientists at the University of Chicago—first by the late Robert Redfield in his several pioneering books on peasant society, and then by Milton Singer in his remarkable study of Indian civilization, *When a Great Tradition Modernizes* (1972). This distinction between the great tradition and the little tradition, between the high culture and the folk culture, has begun to become a commonplace of modern anthropology.

Some of the obvious features of advertising in modern America offer us an opportunity to note the significance or insignificance of that distinction for us. Elsewhere I have tried to point out some of the peculiarities of the American attitude toward the *high* culture. There is something distinctive about the place of thought in American life, which I think is not quite what it has been in certain Old World cultures.

But what about distinctive American attitudes to *popular* culture? What is our analogue to the folk culture of other peoples? Advertising gives us some clues—to a characteristically American democratic folk culture. Folk culture is a name for the culture which ordinary people everywhere lean on. It is not the writings of Dante and Chaucer and Shakespeare and Milton, the teachings of Machiavelli and Descartes, Locke or Marx. It is, rather, the pattern of slogans, local traditions, tales, songs, dances, and ditties. And of course holiday observances. Popular culture in other civilizations has been for the most part both an area of continuity with the past, a way in which people reach back into the past and out to their community, and at the same time an area of local variations. An area of individual and amateur expression in which a person has his own way of saying, or notes his mother's way of saying or singing, or his own way of dancing, his own view of folk wisdom and the cliché.

And here is an interesting point of contrast. In other societies outside the United States, it is the *high* culture that has generally been an area of centralized, organized control. In Western Europe, for example, universities and churches have tended to be closely allied to the government. The institutions of higher learning have had a relatively limited access to the people as a whole. This was inevitable, of course, in most parts of the world, because there were so few universities. In England, for example, there were only two universities until the early nineteenth century. And there was central control over the printed matter that was used in universities or in the liturgy. The government tended to be close to the high culture, and that was easy because the high culture itself was so centralized and because literacy was relatively limited.

In our society, however, we seem to have turned all of this around. Our high culture is one of the least centralized areas of our culture. And our universities express the atomistic, diffused, chaotic, and individualistic aspect of our life. We have in this country more than twenty-five hundred colleges and universities, institutions of so-called higher learning. We have a vast population in these institutions, somewhere over seven million students.

But when we turn to our popular culture, what do we

find? We find that in our nation of Consumption Communities and emphasis on Gross National Product (GNP) and growth rates, advertising has become the heart of the folk culture and even its very prototype. And as we have seen, American advertising shows many characteristics of the folk culture of other societies: repetition, a plain style, hyperbole and tall talk, folk verse, and folk music. Folk culture, wherever it has flourished, has tended to thrive in a limbo between fact and fantasy, and of course, depending on the spoken word and the oral tradition, it spreads easily and tends to be ubiquitous. These are all familiar characteristics of folk culture and they are ways of describing our folk culture, but how do the expressions of our peculiar folk culture come to *us*?

They no longer sprout from the earth, from the village, from the farm, or even from the neighborhood or the city. They come to us primarily from enormous centralized self-consciously *creative* (an overused word, for the overuse of which advertising agencies are in no small part responsible) organizations. They come from advertising agencies, from networks of newspapers, radio, and television, from outdoor-advertising agencies, from the copywriters for ads in the largest-circulation magazines, and so on. These "creators" of folk culture—or pseudo–folk culture—aim at the widest intelligibility and charm and appeal.

But in the United States, we must recall, the advertising folk culture (like all advertising) is also confronted with the problems of self-liquidation and erasure. These are by-products of the expansive, energetic character of our economy. And they, too, distinguish American folk culture from folk cultures elsewhere.

Our folk culture is distinguished from others by being discontinuous, ephemeral, and self-destructive. Where does this leave the common citizen? All of us are qualified to answer.

In our society, then, those who cannot lean on the world of learning, on the high culture of the classics, on the elaborated wisdom of the books, have a new problem. The University of Chicago, for example, in the 1930's and 1940's was the center of a quest for a "common discourse." The champions of that quest, which became a kind of crusade, believed that such a discourse could be found through familiarity with the classics of great literature—and especially of Western European literature. I think they were misled; such works were not, nor are they apt to become, the common discourse of our society. Most people, even in a democracy, and a rich democracy like ours, live in a world of popular culture, our special kind of popular culture.

The characteristic folk culture of our society is a creature of advertising, and in a sense it *is* advertising. But advertising, our own popular culture, is harder to make into a source of continuity than the received wisdom and commonsense slogans and catchy songs of the vivid vernacular. The popular culture of advertising attenuates and is always dissolving before our very eyes. Among the charms, challenges, and tribulations of modern life, we must count this peculiar fluidity, this ephemeral character of that very kind of culture on which other peoples have been able to lean, the kind of culture to which they have looked for the continuity of their traditions, for their ties with the past and with the future.

We are perhaps the first people in history to have a centrally organized mass-produced folk culture. Our kind of popular culture is here today and gone tomorrow—or the day after tomorrow. Or whenever the next semi-annual model appears. And insofar as folk culture becomes advertising, and advertising becomes centralized, it becomes a way of depriving people of their opportunities for individual and small-community expression. Our technology and our economy and our democratic ideals have all helped make that possible. Here we have a new test of the problem that is at least as old as Heraclitus—an everyday test of man's ability to find continuity in his experience. And here democratic man has a new opportunity to accommodate himself, if he can, to the unknown.

TWO

☆ ☆

V

THE PRISON OF THE PRESENT

Our inventive, up-to-the-minute, wealthy democracy makes new tests of the human spirit. Our very instruments of education, of information and of "progress" make it harder every day for us to keep our bearings in the larger universe, in the stream of history and in the whole world of peoples who feel strong ties to their past. A new price of our American standard of living is our imprisonment in the present.

That imprisonment tempts us to a morbid preoccupation with ourselves, and so induces hypochondria. That, the dictionary tells us, is "an abnormal condition characterized by a depressed emotional state and imaginary ill health; excessive worry or talk about one's health." We think we are the beginning and the end of the world. And as a result we get our nation and our lives, our strengths and our ailments, quite out of focus.

We will not be on the way to curing our national hypochondria unless we first see ourselves in history. This requires us to accept the unfashionable possibility that many of our national ills are imaginary and that others may not be as serious as we imagine. Unless we begin to believe that we won't be dead before morning, we may not be up to the daily tasks of a healthy life. By recalling some of the premature obituaries pronounced on other nations, we may listen more skeptically to the moralists and smart alecks who pretend to have in their pocket a life-expectancy chart for nations.

Overwhelmed by the instant moment—headlined in this morning's newspaper and flashed on this hour's newscast—we don't see the whole real world around us. We don't see the actual condition of our long-lived body national.

In a word, we have lost our sense of history. In our schools the story of our nation has been displaced by "social studies"—which is often the story only of what ails us. In our churches the effort to see man *sub specie aeternitatis* has been displaced by a "social gospel"—which is a polemic against the supposed special evils of our time. Our book publishers and literary reviewers no longer seek the timeless and the durable, but spend much of their efforts in fruitless search for à la mode "social commentary"—which they pray won't be out of date when the issue goes to press in two weeks or when the manuscript becomes a book in six months. Our merchandisers frantically devise their semi-annual models which will cease to be voguish when their sequels appear a few months hence. Neither our classroom lessons nor our sermons nor our books nor the things we live with nor the houses we live in are any longer strong ties to our past. We have become a nation of short-term doomsayers.

Without the materials of historical comparison, having lost our traditional respect for the wisdom of ancestors and the culture of kindred nations, we are left with little but abstractions, baseless utopias, to compare ourselves with. No wonder, then, that some of our distraught citizens libel us as the worst nation in the world, or the bane of human history. For we have wandered out of history.

We have nearly lost interest in those real examples from the human past which alone can help us shape standards of the humanly possible. So we compare ours with a mythical Trouble-Free World, where all mankind was at peace. We talk about the war in Vietnam as if it were the first war in American history to which many Americans were opposed. We condemn our nation for not yet having attained perfect justice, and we forget that ours is the most motley and miscellaneous great nation in history—the first to use the full force of law and constitutions and to enlist the vast majority of its citizens in a strenuous quest for justice for all races and ages and religions.

We flagellate ourselves as "poverty-ridden"—by comparison with some mythical time when there was no bottom 20 percent in the economic scale. We sputter against the Polluted Environment—as if it had come with the age of the automobile. We compare our smoggy air not with the odor of horse dung and the plague of flies and the smells of garbage and human excrement which filled cities in the past, but with the honeysuckle perfumes of some nonexistent City Beautiful. We forget that even if the water in many cities today is not as spring-pure nor as palatable as we would like, still for most of history the water of the cities (and of the countryside) was undrinkable. We reproach ourselves for the ills of disease and malnourishment, and forget that until recently, enteritis and measles and whooping cough, diphtheria and typhoid, were killing diseases of childhood, puerperal fever plagued mothers in childbirth, polio was a summer monster.

Flooded by screaming headlines and televised "news" melodramas of dissent, of shrill cries for "liberation," we haunt ourselves with the illusory ideal of some "whole nation" which had a deep and outspoken "faith" in its "values."

We become so obsessed by where we are that we forget where we came from and how we got here. No wonder that we begin to lack the courage to confront the normal ills of modern history's most diverse, growing, burbling Nation of Nations.

Our national hypochondria is compounded by distinctively American characteristics. The American belief in speed, which led us to build railroads farther and faster than any other nation, to invent "quick-lunch" and self-service to save that intolerable ten-minute wait, to build automobiles and highways so we can commute at 70 miles an hour, and which made us a nation of instant cities, instant coffee, and TV dinners, has bred in us a colossal impatience. Any social problem that can't be solved instantly by money and legislation seems fatal. Our appliances and our buildings—and our very lives—seem out of date even before we know it. What can't be done right now seems hardly worth doing at all.

Some of these current attitudes are themselves the late-twentieth-century perversions of the old American Booster Spirit, which has had no precise parallel anywhere else. Totalitarian nations have been marked by their obsession with "planning"—with five-year plans and ten-year plans. But planning expresses willingness to accept a sharp distinction between present and future, between the way things are and the way they might be. And that distinction has never been too popular in the U.S.A. The nineteenth-century Boosters of Western cities defended their extravagant boasts by saying there was no reason to wait, if you were actually bragging only about things that were certain to happen. To them the beauties of Oleopolis or Gopher City were not less real just because they had "not yet gone through the formality of taking place."

This Booster-Vagueness has always made Americans wonderfully unpedantic about the distinction between the present and the future. The amiable vagueness, which once gave an optimistic nineteenth-century America the energy and the hope to go on, still survives. But in a hypochondriac twentieth-century America its effects can be disastrous. Now that very same extravagant vagueness leads some Americans to believe that every battle is Armageddon and that the nation is not less dead just because the national demise also has "not yet gone through the formality of taking place."

An immigrant nation, without an established religion and without political dogma, has had to depend heavily on its sense of a shared past (and a shared future). American history itself was an antidote to dogmatism and utopianism. It proved that a nation did not need to be altogether one thing or another. Federalism was a way of combining local control with national government. Ethnic pluralism was a way of allowing people to keep as much as they wanted of their Old World language, religion, and cuisine—to live among themselves as much as they wished. The immigrant was not compelled either to keep or to abandon his Old World identity. Despite flagrant exceptions expressing prejudices of race, religion, and sex, nevertheless, in the nation as a whole free public schools, and the American innovations of the free high school and the public college, have tried to have standards and yet give everybody the same commodity. The nation aimed to preserve "free private enterprise" (freer and on a larger scale than anywhere else) and yet to provide social security, farm price supports, and other insurance against the free market. On a priori grounds, each and all of these would have seemed impossible, and they were all messy, philosophically speaking.

The best antidote, then, against ruthless absolutes and simple-minded utopias has been American history itself. But that history becomes more and more inaccessible when the technology and institutions of our time imprison us in the present. How can we escape the prison?

First, we must awaken our desire to escape. To do this we must abandon the prevalent belief in the superior wisdom of the ignorant. Unless we give up the voguish reverence for youth and for the "culturally deprived," unless we cease to look to the vulgar community as arbiters of our schools, of our art and literature, and of all our culture, we will never have the will to de-provincialize our minds. We must make every effort to reverse the trend in our schools and colleges—to move away from the "relevant" and toward the cosmopolitanizing, the humanizing, and the unfamiliar. Education is learning what you didn't even know you didn't know. The vogue for "Black Studies" itself grew out of the ghetto, and ironically enough, unwittingly became an effort to idealize the ways of the ghetto. The last thing the able young Negro needs is "Black Studies"—which simply reinforces the unfortunate narrowness of his experience and confines him in *his* provincial present. He does need a better, more cosmopolitan educational system, from kindergarten on up, and a freer opportunity to grasp the opportunities in the whole nation. While he has suffered more than most other Americans from imprisonment in his provincial present, ultimately we all have the same need. We need liberation, too, from the White Ghetto. We all need more ancient history, more medieval history, more of the history and culture of Asia and Africa.

Then, we must enlarge and widen and deepen what we mean by our history. The preoccupation with politics, which has been the bane of the history classroom, fosters unreasonable notions that today governments are the root of all good and evil. The self-righteous effort by self-styled prophets of self-vaunted new "schools" of history would make history a mere tool of contemporary polemics, and so destroy the reason for exploring our past. They would make men of all other ages into the slaves of our conceit—to be used only for our purposes. We must make our history more total by incorporating the past that people lived but that historians have not talked much about. In the United States this means an effort to make more of the history of immigrants, of the history of technology, of the history of everyday life, of business and advertising and housing and eating and drinking and clothing. Democratizing our history does not mean perverting it to the current needs of demagogic or "revolutionary" politics. It does mean enlarging its once-pedantic scope to include the whole spectrum of the ways of life of all men and women and children.

When we allow ourselves to be imprisoned in the present, to be obsessed by the "relevant," we show too little respect for ourselves and our possibilities. We assume that we can properly judge our capacities by the peculiar tests of our own day. But we must look into the whole Historical Catalogue of man's possibilities. To be really persuaded that things can be otherwise, we must see how and when and why they actually have been otherwise.

To revive our sense of history is no panacea for current ills. But it surely is a palliative. It may help us discover what is now curable, may help us define the timetable of the possible, and so help us become something that we are not. If history cannot give us panaceas, it is the best possible cure of the yen for panaceas. And the only proven antidote for utopianism.

"The voice of the intellect," observed Sigmund Freud (who did not underestimate the role of the irrational) in 1928, "is a soft one, but it does not rest until it has gained a hearing. Ultimately, after endlessly repeated rebuffs, it succeeds. This is one of the few points in which one may be optimistic about the future of mankind." Beneath the strident voice of the present we must try to hear the insistent whisper of reason. It does not sound "with it." It speaks only to the attentive listener. It speaks a language always unfamiliar and often archaic. It speaks the language of all past times and places, which is the language of history.

VI

☆ THE NEW REACTIONARIES ☆

The notion seems to have got around that an impartial study of our national past will somehow stand in the way of our future, that the past is the enemy of progress. But by ignoring the path that we have followed, we will be condemned to retrace our steps, and so reenact our struggles. The reactionary, though he may call himself a radical, is the man who refuses to acknowledge history.

An example of our national temptation to become reactionary is the current American attitude toward "minorities" and toward "race." Let me briefly put this in the framework of our history.

In the first place, we must acknowledge that while the record of the American struggle for equality has been impressive and has cheered peoples everywhere, it has also been tragically blotched. While we have been innocent of the worst excesses of overseas colonialism that have been committed by every other modern nation, we were the last modern nation to abolish slavery.

Nearly every group in our country has suffered in its way. Not only the Negroes. "No Irish Need Apply" had its variant somewhere or other for nearly every immigrant. Mexican-Americans were condemned to be peons, Jews suffered from quotas, Japanese, Chinese, Poles, Czechs and Italians, and of course American Indians and all the rest have had their travail. From time to time, national political parties, the Anti-Masons, the Know-Nothings and even sometimes the Democratic and the Republican parties have exploited these prejudices.

But this has not been the mainstream of our history. The great movement of our history has been to bring peoples together—peoples from all social classes, from all continents and all nations. Never before has there been such an international nation. And our history has proved that this was not to be a Diaspora Nation, of peoples in unhappy exile from their homeland, but a nation of peoples reborn. Here Americans found an opportunity to discover themselves as they never could have on the Irish tenant farm, in the Russian ghetto, or in the African village. If this is a textbook cliché, it is nonetheless true.

And if we look for a single word to summarize the special historical relations that came to Old World peoples in this New World, that word is "flow." The United States has been a place of flow—where the peoples and ideas and customs and even the languages of the Old

World have been allowed to flow together. Peoples in more settled continents, rooted in helpless, hopeless serfdom or tenancy, hounded by persecution, confined by ghettos, imprisoned in class and race and national quotas, these peoples came across the ocean in the greatest migration of modern history—fifty million in less than a century. Then millions of those who felt limited and confined on the early-settled Eastern seaboard flowed west across the continent, to unknown and unknowable opportunities. They became the fluid societies of wagon trains, of mining camps, of homestead stakers and city builders—the most fluid societies of modern history.

Flow meant allowing people to discover themselves so that, if they could, they would rise above those who called themselves their "betters." True enough, in much of our century and for most of our history, the barrier of race was almost insuperable and blocked the free flow of Negroes into the more desirable roles in American life. But despite this and some other exceptions, our nation has generally shown a wholesome disrespect for the frozen categories of birth and inherited wealth, and hollow titles and stuffy academies, disrespect for the congenital and the ineradicable, for the honors and the dishonors rooted in ancestry. This is a characteristically American profession, expressed in our Constitution and other national credos.

While the American Revolution and our colonial experience gave us a political federalism, the Great Migrations to our country and across our country in the nineteenth and twentieth centuries brought us a cultural federalism. We could never have become a single nation unless we had recognized the right of Americans to be equal though they be different from one another—in race, in religion, in sex, in wealth, and even in language. While the barrier of race has proven harder than others to surmount, it is plain to the historian that building our nation has meant progressively breaking down the barriers of older worlds. This is the too-easily forgotten meaning of *E pluribus unum*. This is what the Civil War was fought about. It is what generations of Americans—from Dorothea Dix in the early nineteenth century, who struggled to bring the mentally ill into the respectable world, to those who fought for a federal income tax to lower the barriers between rich and poor, to the reformers of our prisons—what all these struggled for.

We must try to keep this story in focus. In our own time, and especially in the last two decades, we have got it out of focus. The new power of minorities, which comes from a hundred potent new forces—from the rise of sociology and the social sciences, to the rise of an assembly-line technology which enables anyone to throw a monkey wrench into the machinery, to the sixty-mile-an-hour superhighway which gives lethal power to anyone who suddenly stops—all this has distorted our view. For the direction of our history was never to give *power* to minorities. The aim, rather, was to break down barriers, and so to allow each of these groups—Negroes, women, young persons, aged persons, or any others—to take their rightful place in the ranks of all Americans. In our tradition, then, despite what some would have us believe, the only truly open Convention of a National Party must be one which knows no quotas, which confines nobody in the numerical boundaries of his race or sex or age. The enemy has not been powerlessness but discrimination. Our historic purpose is to create not a nation of "minorities" but a nation of Americans.

Recently, for the first time in our history, we seem almost to be making an effort to Balkanize this great nation. From the effort to admit more and more Americans to the fellowship of full citizenship and equal opportunity, we seem to have begun to accept as insuperable the barriers which separate our citizens, and even somehow we begin to celebrate them as desirable.

Movements which began in just demands for rights have ended in hollow demands for power. Have we somehow forgotten that our democratic society, as Jefferson and Lincoln preached, was built on the notion that the power of any man over another was itself an evil? Or, in the words of an old common-law maxim, "An equal has no power over an equal." Yet today we risk making power itself into a virtue.

We have forgotten another fact of our history, which should remain a source of pride and should be a guide to our future. The struggle for the equality of Americans has been, in large part, the struggle of some Americans for the rights of *other* Americans. This has been one of the great unifiers of our nation. A half-million Americans (most of them not Negroes) died in a civil war to abolish the slavery of Negroes. Of course we have also known the politics of interest groups and of regions. Our legislatures act with the aid and guidance (and sometimes the misguidance) of lobbyists; political causes thrive from those whom they will profit. But the great chapters in our history have been written by those who tried to improve the lot of other and all Americans. The wealthy Theodore Roosevelt wielded a big stick to protect the little American against the excesses of large corporations; the wealthy Franklin Roosevelt espoused the cause of the poor and the unemployed; a General of the Army, Dwight D. Eisenhower, championed civilian control of the Armed Forces. The struggle for the civil rights of Negroes was long financed and encouraged mainly by Jews and Catholics and Protestants, by Americans of all other races. And, of course, we must remember that the constitutional amendment which gave the vote to women was enacted by a nation of nonfemale voters.

There is something noble about struggling for the rights of others, but it is merely human to fight in self-defense. A dangerous clue to our loss of historical bearings is our willingness not only to tolerate but even to admire self-defense groups which confuse their own power with the public welfare. The politics of narrow self-seeking groups is only a little removed from the morality of every-man-for-himself. When before has it been respectable for American politicians to declare themselves the candidates for their race, for Americans to accept uncritically a racial caucus in the Congress of the nation? Is a Black Caucus any more respectable than a White Caucus? In the past, with few exceptions, American politicians have been ashamed to call themselves the candidate of only one group of citizens. They have found it necessary at least to pretend to represent all their constituents equally.

We need a new direction in our public consciousness to help us move further toward fulfilling the American mission for man. We can rediscover that direction in our history.

We must return to the ideal of equality. We must recognize that many of the acts committed in the name of equal opportunity are in fact acts of discrimination. We must reject reactionary programs, though they masquerade under slogans of progress, which would carry us back to Old World prejudices, primitive hatreds, and discriminatory quotas. Our cultural federalism, another name for the fellowship of man in America, must once again emphasize what each can give to us. We must reject the clenched fist for the open hand. We must aim, more than ever before, to become color-blind. We must aim to create conditions of equal opportunity—by improving American schools beginning at the very bottom, and by ruthlessly applying the same standards of achievement to all Americans regardless of race, sex, religion, or national origin—the same standards for admission to institutions of higher learning, for graduation, for the Civil Service, for elected office, and for all other American opportunities. We weaken our nation and show disrespect for all our fellow Americans when we make race or sex or poverty a disqualification—and equally so when we make them a qualification.

A more open America is a nation with fewer barriers. It is not a nation of proud, chauvinistic, self-seeking "minorities." We must not allow ourselves to become the Quota States of America.

VII

THE LANDSCAPE OF DEMOCRACY

Just as our society has its own way of looking at the past and of placing people in the flow of history, so we have our way of viewing and shaping the landscape. We can begin to define this landscape of American democracy by contrasting another sort of landscape.

Adolf Hitler's architect, Albert Speer, who ran Nazi munitions production during World War II, in the vivid memoirs written during his twenty-five years in Spandau Prison, leaves us a catalog of alien attitudes. In 1934 Hitler assigned Speer the task of building a grand new stadium for Nazi Party rallies on Zeppelin Field at Nuremberg. The attractive young Speer, then only twenty-nine years old, set out to sate Hitler's architectural megalomania. Hoping to become the architect laureate of the Nazis, Speer expounded to Hitler "A Theory of Ruin Value":

> The idea was that buildings of modern construction were poorly suited to form that "bridge of tradition" to future generations which Hitler was calling for. It was hard to imagine that rusting heaps of rubble [like those which remained when they demolished the Nuremberg streetcar depot to make way for the new stadium] could communicate these heroic inspirations which Hitler admired in the monuments of the past. My "theory" was intended to deal with this dilemma. By using special materials and by applying certain principles of statics, we should be able to build structures which even in a state of decay, after hundreds or (such were our reckonings) thousands of years would more or less resemble Roman models.
>
> To illustrate my ideas I had a romantic drawing prepared. It showed what the reviewing stand on the Zeppelin Field would look like after generations of neglect, overgrown with ivy, its columns fallen, the walls crumbling here and there, but the outlines still clearly recognizable. In Hitler's entourage this drawing was regarded as blasphemous. That I could even conceive of a period of decline for the newly founded Reich destined to last a thousand years seemed outrageous to many of Hitler's closest followers. But he himself accepted my ideas as logical and illuminating. He gave orders that in the future the important buildings of his Reich were to be erected in keeping with the principles of this "law of ruins."

Speer's grandiose, apocalyptic view of the nation, its buildings, and their future expressed the hollow and reckless Nazi view of man and society. Other societies, less naïvely and less obviously, express their own attitudes to public buildings and historical monuments.

Our American society, too, has found its way. There is a Landscape of American Democracy, which gives a special place and a special role to our buildings (especially our public buildings) very different from that envisioned by Hitler and the Nazis. It is also different from the landscapes shaped by the aristocratic traditions of Western Europe, or by the totalitarian dogmas of Eastern Europe.

Aristocratic societies with long histories automatically produce historical monuments. The American traveler visiting the most interesting attractions in England, France, Italy, Spain, or Germany, will spend his time in palaces and castles and forts, and if he goes to museums, they will often be palaces or castles adapted to this new purpose. The Louvre, for example, was originally built as a royal fortress and palace by Philip II about 1204, was reconstructed under a commission from Francis I after 1545, opened as a public museum in 1793, and then was proclaimed the Musée Napoléon in 1803. In Florence the Uffizi Gallery, originally built by Vasari to serve Cosimo de Medici as public offices (i.e., *uffizi*), has had a comparable variegated career. The splendid durable residences of the rich and wellborn were, by definition, the seats of rule.

Yet many of the most impressive monuments of earlier ages have proved almost as useful to later ages as ruins as they were when they functioned as buildings. Albert Speer had a point. For twentieth-century chauvinists and megalomaniacs, myth-rich ruins can sometimes serve better than a well-preserved original. Mussolini (who wanted a prod to national pride) found a crumbling Forum in Rome perhaps better for his purposes than a working model would have been. What he needed was not so much a reminder of surviving glories as a token of the bygone glories that a once-imperial people must fight to recapture.

Of course, there have been some novel problems for the communists and for some other recent totalitarians who wish to make monuments serve their propaganda. In the Soviet Union, for example, churches have been preserved (and even refurbished) as museums of antireligion. The ideologues who establish the government policy that the past and the traditional are by definition evil, fear the beauty of everything ancient. They therefore try to exhibit the splendor of earlier times in such a way as to disgust and disenchant. There is evidence that these efforts are less than entirely successful, and sometimes even backfire.

Some characteristic American ways of viewing the monumental past are so obvious that they may have escaped our notice. Here are a few.

1. *The American urban landscape has generally been dominated not by public, ecclesiastical, or government buildings, but by semipublic monuments of business enterprise, industry, and community pride.* While the focus in the landscape of Old World cities was commonly government structures, churches, or the residences of rulers, the landscape and the skyline of American cities have boasted their hotels, department stores, office buildings, apartments, and skyscrapers. In this grandeur, Americans have expressed their Booster Pride, their hopes for visitors and new settlers, and customers, for thriving commerce and industry. The skyscraper-castellated cores of American cities, with Walt Dis-

neyesque clarity, have symbolized the American confusion of present and future. In them we see the optimistic, sometimes megalomaniac vision of the Go-Getters who built the enterprises that built the buildings, or who built the buildings to house the enterprises: the visions of a John Wanamaker, an F. W. Woolworth, a Henry Hyde, or a Conrad Hilton, among many others.

2. *Inevitably, then, in the United States past monuments, however grand, have commonly been removed to make way for those still grander.* The good is removed to make way for the new, the big is rcmovcd to make way for the bigger. Many edifices of past aristocratic cultures—meant to be used only by a lucky, happy few—survived intact because they were *not* used by a numerous indiscriminate public. Some of them (for example, the buildings currently serving as national museums in Portugal) were haphazardly preserved precisely because they were useful to so many different purposes and regimes. But our democratic past uses up, improves, and replaces. The great American contribution to domestic architecture—the balloon-frame house—was quick to put up, required little skill, and could be demounted and made portable.

Our conspicuous architectural successes and our great efforts, unlike those of aristocratic or government-dominated cultures, have been in the improvement of domestic construction, in the building of large semipublic structures—factories, apartment buildings, housing developments, hotels, and office buildings—mainly with private resources from private enterprise. Our schools have been built mostly with local funds and around local ideas, our universities and museums and libraries have in large part been the contribution of private individuals, built not on the scheme of some emperor, or dictator, or minister of public works, but around the ideas of some local community and of people devoted to that particular community.

Democratic successes have been successes in way of life for the millions. And as these ways improve, as old buildings are torn down to make way for new, what is left is an American democratic landscape with few relics of the past. It is significant that downtown Chicago, the headquarters and laboratory of American urban architecture, now exhibits so few reminders of Louis Sullivan, Frank Lloyd Wright, and the other pioneers who did much of their great work there. Their buildings were regularly replaced by "better"—or at least bigger—buildings. Occasional relics of their genius (like Sullivan's Auditorium) have been preserved through the strenuous, and sometimes unpopular, efforts of private individuals who have been willing to be called enemies of progress. As Carl Sandburg urged (in "The Windy City"): "Put the city up; tear the city down; put it up again; let us find a city." Some Chicago boosters considered the Great Chicago Fire of 1871 (which cleared the architectural decks in a vast area of the city center) a providential stroke, since it happily opened a path for the future. In other, smaller cities (Tulsa, Oklahoma, for example) recent visitors have been astonished to find new skyscrapers rising downtown, only a few blocks from slightly less new, only slightly lower skyscrapers which were largely unoccupied.

The Urban Renewal movement has been ruthless and reckless in leveling monuments of the past. The Urban Rot at the core of our great cities is a disease often produced by buildings that were larger and grander than the needs of their generation. And Urban Blight (shamefully displayed in the heart of the national capital by the long-unused, architecturally delightful Willard Hotel, and with counterparts in other cities across the continent) is a symptom of a people's unwillingness or inability to adapt old structures to new ones. If we can't tear it down, we leave it there to rot.

Many of our handsomest, most history-laden structures stand empty and useless. Ghost cities—twentieth-century versions of the nineteenth-century ghost town—deface our urban landscape. Meanwhile glossy, gaudy, huge new shopping centers, office buildings, and skyscraper-motels spring up on the outskirts.

3. *The present is the climax of our history*. Many of our disappointments come from our feeling that we always have a right to expect the American present to be grander, richer, more adventurous, and perhaps even more virtuous than all our past American eras. Or, in Abraham Lincoln's phrase that the United States is the "last best hope of earth." This was the come-on to immigrants from the whole world. It is the appeal of the annual model, and of the latest model of anything and everything. In the United States, as in few other times or places, "newest" is a synonym for "best." Yet, unlike some other nations born in revolutions or so-called revolutions, we claim a constitutional progressivism. Our American Revolution was supposed to be, and is still assumed to have been, a fulfillment of all past aspirations, including the best of the old English Bill of Rights, of the British Constitution and the ancient common law. Our present thus boasts a continuity with the past: the latest version of anything is supposed to include all the best

features of the old reliable. So we don't drop a tear for lost empires or past glories. There has been no American Ozymandias.

In our landscape of democracy, then, physical, monumental ties to the past are precious few. We are not rich in the means to stir our sense of continuity with our past. It is not easy to find the signs to remind ourselves that the nation was not born yesterday. We are peculiarly ill equipped with remembrancers.

There are a number of obvious ways in which we supply self-consciously some of the remembrancing resources which other nations receive as an effortless legacy. Many of these institutions, widespread in other countries, take on a peculiar significance for us. And some of them flourish here as never before. Museums of art, of history, of science, and of technology—the traditional avenues to the past—have grown and spread across the country with a prolific vigor. Our more than six thousand museums, in numbers, in quality, and in the devotion of their local supporters, are comparable to our institutions of higher learning. They range from the great National Museums of the Smithsonian Institution in the capital, and the famous metropolitan museums in New York City, Chicago, Cleveland, Los Angeles, and elsewhere, to admirable museums in our colleges and universities, and to the small but respectable museums of local historical societies, art associations, industries, and countless other groups. There are the great restorations and re-creations—including those at Colonial Williamsburg, New Salem, Mystic, Old Sturbridge, and Greenfield Village—and the many historical parks of the National Park Service. Then there are the preservations—Mount Vernon, Monticello, Gunston Hall, and scores of other buildings—whose survival and accessibility for the public depend on the enthusiasm and energy of local associations. There are, of course, the Library of Congress, the National Archives, and the increasing number of presidential libraries and museums across the country. And besides, there are historical sites—like Andalusia, Nicholas Biddle's grand estate outside Philadelphia—which enlightened private owners make accessible to the public. Most obvious, of course, are the monuments which were built to be monuments—Bunker Hill Monument, the Washington Monument, the Lincoln Memorial, and others—which still impress us.

There is, however, one kind of relationship to the past in which our landscape is peculiarly lacking. Where are our remembrancers of the continuous, usable past? While most other peoples live among vivid daily reminders of the useful legacy of earlier generations, such reminders become every day more uncommon in our annual-modeled, mobile America. Those thriving and proliferating self-conscious efforts which I have just mentioned, to preserve and display relics of the past, in their very way of recalling our past also somehow remind us that the past is something we usually bypass or discard. They tell us, by implication, that we must make a special effort to recover relics from the past—the world of the obsolete and the outmoded. Of course, there are local and regional exceptions—in Boston, Charleston, or St. Augustine, in occasional villages in New England and the South and elsewhere, and in carefully preserved, historic family residences. Such sites and buildings are concentrated in a few areas along the Atlantic seaboard, in the original thirteen colonies, in Texas, and in California. They are commonly associated with an interest in genealogy, with an ancestor pride and a hereditary snobbery quite uncharacteristic of our national life.

For the nation as a whole, national remembrancers of the usable past are precious few. And the scarcity of others may help explain that American reverence for the federal Constitution which foreigners find hard to understand. Among the few physical reminders of useful continuity with our national past two are of special interest.

One is what remains of the American wilderness. Some of this is still preserved in our National Parks, National Forests and Wilderness Areas, and in the State Parks. Because of the very brevity of American history, because American civilization was "an Errand into the Wilderness," because this new nation succeeded in making over a savage landscape into an industrial society, the wilderness in America tells here what it tells nowhere else. While in England or France or Germany the remaining wilderness is a refuge from history, in the United States our wilderness is a vivid reminder of our history. In this sense, *all* the National Parks, and especially the wilderness parks, are characteristically American national *historical* parks. And even if the preservation of these areas were not essential for recreation and as a refuge from the city into nature, they would be peculiarly necessary as still-useful (and every year more necessary) reminders of our all-American past. Among the many ironies of American history, none is more remarkable than that now we must make strenuous, organized efforts to preserve that very wilderness which it was so long the aim (at great cost in life and treasure) of American pioneers to conquer and abolish.

A very special American reminder of the usable past is the national capitol. Other nations, of course, have their capitol buildings, their gathering places for representatives or delegates from the whole nation. But in addition to the reasons I have already mentioned, there are some features of modern American life which give our national capitol building in Washington a poignant significance, both in what it does and in what it symbolizes.

The national capitol holds a unique place in the landscape of democracy. For the United States has been a new name for new and unpredictable ways of finding substitutes and alternatives to the past. The whole cast of American life has been against preservation, against conservation of the old. Where, then, can we, as a nation, be reminded of our paternity, of our oneness with the past?

The national capitol plays a unique role as a remembrancer. In a nation that views its past not as a series of remote and glorious islands, but as a stream that feeds the present, and which finds innumerable reasons to level the physical reminders of the past, there is no substitute for the Capitol. Not only because of its antiquity (by American standards) but also and especially because it has remained in continuous use since its construction and because it remains the center of the representative function of our national government. President Washington, to the accompaniment of Masonic ceremonies, laid the cornerstone of the Capitol Building on September 18, 1793. The great cast-iron dome, which unifies the whole structure (on a plan borrowed from Michelangelo's design for St. Peter's in Rome and from Sir Christopher Wren's design for St. Paul's in London), was begun in 1856 and completed in 1865—the very years of the war for national union.

The tendencies of modern American life, including our great successes, and especially the technological successes of our day, will make the monumental and symbolic role of the United States Capitol even more necessary in the coming decades. American technology, and especially television, has dispersed our people, segregated our audiences into one's and two's and three's. Face-to-face gatherings of numerous citizens have become fewer and less important than ever before. For this reason, the opportunity to attend gatherings for sports events are valued perhaps more than ever, for they remain among the rare occasions on which we can satisfy a common human need.

The United States Capitol, however, has been continuously used as a place where our public men have gathered for face-to-face meetings to do the nation's business and formulate our hopes and purposes. It remains a symbol of the too-fast-waning belief that there is no substitute for the human presence, no substitute for congregation. The Capitol is our insurance against the peril (we may laugh at it, but others have laughed too soon at more unlikely inventions) that ways will be found for congressmen to "meet" without their even being there. Then why should they not remain in their offices in their separate constituencies and have their meetings by remote control? We must pray against that day.

These tendencies of modern technology, along with the

refinements of the techniques of opinion polling, have seduced our political scientists to overemphasize the tie from the Congress back to the voter and not to give enough attention to another aspect of the Congress. That is, the relationship of congressmen to one another. Yet it is in the daily meetings and working together in the Capitol that they really activate the democratic spirit. There they justify the interest, the worries, the hopes of their constituents. They serve their wider constituency—the nation—by how they behave to one another.

The United States Capitol, then, as the national meeting house of American democracy, takes on a newly required role as a symbol of the deliberative functions of our Congress. The Capitol can remind us as no other symbol can that by our ballots what we create is not a random list of spokesmen for district constituencies, but a *congregation.* In the Capitol our representatives' highest duty is to meet, deliberate, persuade, discuss, compromise with, and encourage one another. In this forum, expressions of disrespect for fellow members are out of order. Here the need for decision, and the uncertainties of whose support may be needed next week, enforce decency, sympathy, human warmth—into a working liberalism.

In this century the techniques of market research, supported by large-scale enterprise and advertising, have been elaborated into the science of opinion polling and then further refined into techniques for opening channels between the members of Congress and their constituents. Never before have our representatives possessed such effective means for testing the opinions, prejudices, and changing preferences of the voters back home. And our political scientists, with the help of a new breed of interpretive reporters, of whom Theodore H. White and Samuel Lubell are brilliant examples, have focused as never before on the shifts of opinion among voters, and on how, when, and why they change their attitude toward their representatives. Of course, no prudent politician would neglect any means for discovering what the voters want. But we have all been tempted to give undue emphasis to this aspect of the congressman's job, to the ties from Washington back to the voter.

With the rise of voter science ("psephology" is its barbarous new name), the growth of opinion polling, and the increasing dominance of radio and television in campaigning, we have tended to give less attention to a proper traditional role of the Congress. The sessions of Congress (excepting only inaugurations, presidential addresses, and emergency sessions) remain among the few gatherings of public significance in the nation which do not now appear on television.

Our deliberative, congregated Congress, with its remarkable traditions of mutual respect among members, and its astonishing decorum (by contrast with the deliberative bodies of many other republics), remains our refuge from the perils of mob rule, from the dictatorship of popular passions. So long as there is a United States Capitol and it is being conscientiously used by an actual congregation of our representatives, we will have some insurance against the excesses of democracy, and against some other excesses as well. We will have a reassurance that we are trying to use all the resources of the mind, of the human presence and personality, to preserve a constitutional democracy and, in every generation, to improve its institutions.

The hilltop site which was to be occupied by the Capitol Building was described in 1796 by L'Enfant, planner of the city of Washington, D.C., as "a pedestal waiting for a monument." That monument is still being built, and in every generation will be rebuilt. For it is a monument to our oneness with our past, and to the continuing efforts of always-changing congregations of Americans to discover new meanings for democracy in every generation.

THREE

☆ ☆

VIII

☆ THE EXPLORING SPIRIT ☆

In America, exploration and growth have been synonymous. We have been an exploring nation, for the settlement of our nation, unlike others, has been contemporaneous with the exploring of our land. The frontier which many have used as a hallmark of our history has been simply another name for the boundaries of the unknown. Much of the greatness, the optimism, the energy and the boldness of our country has come from this peculiar way of growing. In fact, the people who built America were not afraid to plunge into the unknown, to live on the edge of the unknown.

We are prone to forget some of the special characteristics of their experience. First, the uncertainty and the willingness to take risks. This was a meaning of the New World.

When the Puritans came here from England and from Holland they moved to the edge of mystery. When people moved westward in the wagon trains in the nineteenth century, they moved across the unknown. When immigrants came from the countries of Europe in the nineteenth century, they moved into a world they did not know.

The exploration of this unknown was undertaken in community. From Columbus in the late fifteenth century, who came with his scores of fellows, down to the westward-moving wagon trains in the mid-nineteenth century, people organized themselves together to move more swiftly and more safely. The same was true of those who built the fur trade and their many followers who developed American enterprise. All these pioneers helped make it socially and spiritually possible for us to undertake our space explorations. Our classic American enterprises have been undertaken by large numbers of people organized and effective together.

The exploring spirit has expressed faith in the unpredicted and the unpredictable. Its theological form was a not-merely-ritual expression of belief in Divine Providence uttered again and again by George Washington and by his successors in the Presidency. It was once said that the best evidence that a Divine Providence watched over the American people was the Presidents whom the American people have survived. This was said, by the way, at the time of the election of Abraham Lincoln. The secular form of this faith in the unpredicted and the unpredictable was the Booster Spirit. Americans have been willing to buy stock in the future and to postpone benefits—partly because our American future has always seemed to merge so conveniently into our American present. All this expresses our sanguine determination not to be afraid to detail the grand American future simply because it is not yet here.

The American nation has grown, for the most part, not by conquest but by exploration. But the modern nations which built empires in the recent centuries have based them mostly on conquest. The Spanish, the Portuguese, the Dutch, the French, the British, and the German empires were efforts to grow and become powerful by adding areas of known value which would produce known commodities. In England, for example, at the end of the French and Indian War in 1763, there was a large party which preferred to take the two tiny islands of Guadeloupe from the French in place of Canada because Guadeloupe was a known quantity producing valuable tropical goods and Canada was a massive unknown. The United States, however, has grown by exploring, by discovering the values in a new world and in unknown areas.

Much of the vitality of American civilization in our century will depend on our ability to translate this exploring spirit, this enthusiasm for the unknown, into late-twentieth-century terms. This is not easy to do. We see some evidences of it in the spectacular recent growth of "Research and Development." Now "R & D," which has become a major enterprise of American business, is really a symbol in the world of industry of our quest for the unknown and the unpredicted.

But at the same time many of the peculiar influences in American civilization in our day—in fact the very successes of American civilization in the twentieth century—

have tended to dampen or dilute the exploring spirit. The fantastic and unpredictable successes of our civilization have, among other effects, produced the following consequences in our daily lives.

First, there has been what I would call "the neutralization of risks." Some of the more obvious factors in this have been the growth of welfare government and the improvement of medicine and public health. A symbol of the neutralization of risks which has not been sufficiently noted has been the rise of insurance: unemployment insurance, health insurance, and (less noticed, although psychologically of equal importance) casualty insurance. The history of American casualty insurance—the means by which Americans protect themselves from the risks of their daily lives—begins as recently as 1864 when the Travelers Insurance Company was formed to issue travel accident policies. When, in 1868, a casualty insurance company began to inspect steam boilers, they pioneered modern techniques of loss prevention and helped develop new ways of indemnifying industrial enterprises for accidents. By 1898 there were fourteen companies sharing casualty premiums of some $11 million; by 1960 there were thirty-five hundred companies with total premiums of over $9 billion a year. The rise and diffusion of compulsory insurance in many forms, including "no-fault" insurance, is only the latest longest step. The effect of all this has been to encourage Americans to think that they can remove or at least reduce most of the risks of daily life.

At the same time the triumphs of American industry have led to the decline of the miraculous. We have seen the erasing of regions in food, the erasing of seasons in our diet, by the rise of canning, refrigeration, and deep-freezing; then, too, the erasing of seasonal climates by central heating, and in our time by air conditioning. Finally, the erasing of space itself by air transport and radio and television has further eroded our sense of the miraculous. Now with television, it is possible for us to be more there when we are here than when we are there.

An additional development of our industrial world has been the rise of repeatable experience: the new and ever-increasing opportunity to replay all the events of the past. It had its beginning with photography in the middle of the nineteenth century, advanced with the development of the phonograph and the motion picture, and has climaxed with kinescoping and instant replay, which has done much to remove the spontaneity even of sports experiences.

Finally, as a result of these and other factors there has been the crowding of the continent. The global view closes in. We must go in search of wilderness, which is another name for the unpredicted and the uncontrollable. A consequence of all this in our time has been a certain flattening of experience—a dilution of the sense of spontaneous adventure. Even words lose their exciting old meanings. When we are told that a new real estate development will be "An Adventure in Suburban Living" we are supposed to know exactly what to expect. Is this—the fulfillment of advertised expectations—what we mean by "adventure" today?

We note everywhere a decline of the risky, a decline of the unpredicted, a decline of the unknown. But space exploring can keep alive and stimulate the traditional American exploring spirit, can help remind us of this spirit and can develop our pride in that spirit. The uncertainties, the risks and the hopes of space exploring can help us keep alive some of our oldest traditions: the traditions of community, the tradition of risk-taking, of unknown-seeking. It can dramatize all our community efforts, for our moon shots are, of course, the greatest focused collaborative exploring efforts in history.

In our paradoxical nation, no paradox is more intriguing than the combination of our pragmatic spirit with our love affair with the unknown. It is appropriate that our new world should be the point of takeoff for newer worlds. By moving into outer space we can effect a change in mankind's point of view, we can lift man above the petrified world he knows, much as did Copernicus and his followers and the explorers to America in shifting from the geocentric to the heliocentric point of view. Now we direct man's view toward the new continents of outer space in the discovery of new Americas.

Just as the shift which came with the discovery and settlement of America changed Old World thinking about the world and at the same time provided a new locus of experience, so will space exploring. It will keep alive and vigorous, dramatically and symbolically clear, the exploring spirit which is the American mission. What might be the meaning of that mission for all of us was suggested by T. S. Eliot, a questing American refugee from American civilization:

We shall not cease from exploration
And the end of all our exploring
Will be to arrive where we started
And know the place for the first time.

IX

SELF-LIQUIDATING  IDEALS 

Worrying about our values is more than a characteristic headache of our time. It is a by-product of long and potent forces in our history and of many peculiarities of American life. More perhaps than any other people, we Americans have tended to talk and think or (more precisely) to worry about our values. In our own time this tendency is a by-product of the American concept of a standard of living, of the American attitude to technology and of American success in technology. We can better understand (though I suspect we can never cure) this American habit if we notice a peculiarity of the ideals to which we have been led by our geography, our wealth, our know-how, and our history.

We Americans have been led to the pursuit of some self-liquidating ideals. Myriad circumstances of our history have led us in this direction. A self-liquidating ideal is an ideal which is dissolved in the very act of fulfillment. Many of our most prominent and dominant ideals have had just this quality.

The earliest example is in the very first appeal of America—as a new world. The first charm of the continent was its newness. But when the new nation in a new world flourished and endured, it became old. By the later twentieth century we were among the oldest of the new nations of modern times. Our federal Constitution, which in 1787 seemed so uncertain an experiment, is now the oldest written Constitution in working order.

How to stay young? This problem plagues nations as well as individuals. But it plagues us more than other nations.

How can we keep alive the experimental spirit, the verve and vitality, the adventure-lovingness of youth? Nations which glory in their antiquity—an Italy which traces its founders back and into the heavens to Romulus and Remus, the twin sons of Mars, and to a semimythic Aeneas; a France which reaches back to a Saint Louis and Saint Joan; a Britain whose genealogy includes a legendary King Arthur—those nations have other special problems. Despite occasional revolutions and pretended revolutions, in modern times those nations, even when they have gloried in newness, have tried to sanctify it with the aura of antiquity. They have aimed to historicize their myths.

Our nation, founded in the glaring light of history, from the beginning set itself a task of renewal. Our Pilgrim Fathers and Founding Fathers hoped to give the men of older worlds a second chance. But could any world—even this brave New World—stay forever new?

It is not only this first and most obvious of American ideals which has seemed to be self-liquidating. The newness of our nation would come, we were told, from the fact that the United States would be as varied and as multiplex as mankind. We would be (in Whitman's phrase) "a Nation of Nations." Our nation was to be (as Emma Lazarus proclaimed in her inscription on the base of the Statue of Liberty)

> Mother of Exiles. From her beacon-hand
> Glows world-wide welcome. . . .

The whole earth would be our womb. Our wealth and strength would be in our variety.

Of course, there were other regions of the world—the Balkans, the Middle East, South Asia—which also were a mélange of peoples and languages and religions. What would distinguish the United States was that we would give our varied peoples the opportunity to become one. As they were dissolved in the American "melting pot" they would become part of a single community.

But suppose we actually succeeded. Suppose we brought all the immigrant world into one great new nation. Suppose we managed to Americanize and assimilate the varied peoples of the world. What then?

Inevitably—and ironically—success would mean a new homogeneity. If the nation really succeeded in drawing together all these peoples, giving them a chance to discover their common humanity and to forget the feuds and ancient hatreds that had held them apart, how could it fail to dissolve much of that rich variety, that pungency which itself justified building a "Nation of Nations"?

This danger was not purely theoretical. The nineteenth century, which brought us tens of millions of varied immigrants—from Ireland, Italy, Poland, the Balkans, the Middle East, and elsewhere—concluded in a paroxysm of fear and puzzlement. Old settlers (themselves, of course, descended from immigrant Americans), once they became comfortable here, began to fear that the nation might not be homogeneous enough. The Immigration Restriction League, founded in the 1890's by a group of bright Harvard graduates, soon included many of the nation's most respectable political leaders, industrialists, labor leaders, educators, scholars, and authors. Congressional hearings on the "problem" of immigration then produced forty-odd published volumes on the evils of immigration. The popular "remedy" for the nation's variety was to assimilate the immigrant, and different ethnic groups were rated according to the ease and speed with which they "became" American. The new immigration policy of the 1920's proclaimed the dissolving of the adventurously pluralist ideal.

The pluralist ideal was being abandoned, not merely because some people believed it was wrong, or that it could never succeed. A better explanation of what was happening was that the effort to build a strong, nationalist, community-conscious people from this international miscellany had substantially succeeded. Millions, whose immigrant parents had arrived within the preceding century, came to believe in a newly consolidated Americanism, which left no place for later immigrants—or for others who were conspicuously, if superficially, unlike themselves. The organized labor movement, which included immigrants and was led by immigrants and the children of immigrants, had joined with New England bluebloods to demand an end to the opportunities for others which had made their own lives possible.

The years from about 1880 to about 1930 witnessed the greatest confusion in the shaping of an American ideal of nationhood. First- and second-generation immigrants collaborated with the descendants of earlier, more respectable and more prosperous immigrants, to define 100 percent Americanism. At the same time a new American sociology, which was substantially a Science of Minorities, arose to give respectability and aggressiveness to pluralism.

By the 1930's many Americans had moved from the older ideal of assimilation ("Americanize the immigrant") to the newer ideal of integration (allow each group to remain integral, and to glory in its distinctness). That was the first heyday of the balanced ticket. It was the age of the second Ku Klux Klan, with its white racism and anti-Semitism and anti-Catholicism. And, in response, it became an age of aggressive ethnicity. The grandchildren of immigrants, in search of their roots, fabricated a newly assertive and chauvinistic sense of separateness. Many otherwise respectable Americans were surprisingly tolerant of the racism of the Ku Klux Klan. This confusion survives into our own age, and helps explain the aggressive ethnicity and racism of groups like the Black Panthers, and the shocking toleration of destructive and illegal acts committed under the cover of racial separatism. The battle over immigration left scars among ethnic minorities not unlike the sectional scars left by the Civil War.

How can we fulfill the American ideal of pluralism without liquidating it? If we build a single strong "Nation of Nations," will not our nationality inevitably overshadow our ethnicity? When we must (however facetiously) urge our fellow Americans to "Be Ethnic," do we not declare that the price of success in our pluralistic nation has been to make us less plural? Perhaps some of the ethnic pangs of our age come from the discovery that this cherished ideal may be self-liquidating.

Other examples of our self-liquidating American ideals arise from our success in building a high standard of living, from our efforts to bring the best material things to everybody. "Every man a King"—Huey Long's extravagant slogan—is not far from the sober American hope. When before has a nation set itself the ideal of bringing to every citizen the delights of advanced technology?

I will offer two commonplace examples of how we have tended to be frustrated by our remarkable success in approaching this ideal.

1. *A Wilderness Holiday for Everybody: the Problem of our National Parks.* There is no more distinctive or more successful American institution than our National Parks. The National Park Service, within the Department of Interior, has demonstrated an efficiency, an imagination, and a democratic largeness of spirit to inspire all of us. Yet, despite their best efforts, and even because of their brilliant success, we face here again the troublesome paradox.

A purpose of our National Parks, beginning with the establishment of Yellowstone National Park in 1872, has been to preserve our wilderness for the benefit of all the American people. Rocky Mountain National Park, Grand Teton National Park, Glacier National Park, Yellowstone, and Yosemite, among others, aim to make accessible to all Americans the delights of the pristine continent. Our National Parks now comprise over fifteen million acres and receive some fifty-four million visitors each year. Their reach to the American public would have been impossible, of course, without the American Standard of Living, which includes the improvement and diffusion of the automobile, an unexcelled network of highways, and a high standard of leisure, with regular and extensive paid vacations.

The National Parks, themselves part of the American Standard of Living, have made it possible to democratize the wilderness. An American, then, does not need to be wealthy, to own a large estate, or to afford a retinue of servants to reach and enjoy thousands of acres of the most remote, most unspoiled, and most spectacular landscapes in the nation.

But, as Robert Cahn of *The Christian Science Monitor* has asked, "Will success spoil the national parks?" Our wilderness acres, simply because they are so attractive and so accessible, have begun to become traffic jams. Living conditions in the campsites of Yosemite Valley and around Lake Yellowstone—with laundry lines hanging from tent to tent and one camper unwittingly putting his elbow in his neighbor's soup—begin to resemble the congested cities from which these campers have fled. In 1967, for example, serious crimes in National Parks rose 67 percent, compared with a 16 percent rise in the crime rate in American cities.

The democratization of the automobile and the democratization of the wilderness countryside threaten to destroy the very landscapes that we want everybody to have access to. Is a wilderness holiday for all Americans a self-liquidating ideal?

2. *The Democracy of Things: From Model T to the Annual Model.* Henry Ford's dream was to make a new and better kind of family horse—a car which everybody could afford and which would last forever. Essential to his plan, of course, was perfecting his Model T. Although he was experimental in developing his car, he believed that once the design was fixed, the object was simply to find ways to make it by the millions.

It was essential to his ideal that all the cars should be alike. As he saw it, mass production (what he called "the democratization of the automobile") required standardization, and standardization meant turning out a single uniform product. "The way to make automobiles," Henry Ford explained in 1903, "is to make one automobile like another automobile, to make them all alike, to make them come through the factory just alike; just as one pin is like another pin when it comes from a pin factory, or one match is like another when it comes from a match factory."

To Ford this meant finding ways to turn out millions of Model T's. He was confident that he could succeed. In 1909 a friend warned Ford that the automobile would create a "social problem" by frightening all the horses on the highway. "No, my friend," Ford replied, "you're mistaken. I'm not creating a social problem at all. I am going to democratize the automobile. When I'm through everybody will be able to afford one, and about everyone will have one. The horse will have disappeared from our highways, the automobile will be taken for granted, and there won't be any problem."

Toward this end Ford focused his efforts on making his car as cheap as possible, making repairs inexpensive and easy. He continued to believe it was his mission to mass-produce copies of the same durable product. In 1922 he still insisted:

> We cannot conceive how to serve the consumer unless we make for him something that, as far as we can provide, will last forever. We want to construct some kind of machine that will last forever. It does not please us to have a buyer's car wear out or become obsolete. We want the man who buys one of our products never to have to buy another. We never make an improvement that renders any previous model obsolete. The parts of a specific model are not only interchangeable with similar parts on all other cars of that model, but they are interchangeable with similar parts on all the cars that we have turned out.

He meant what he said, and he had the power to make his dream come true.

Ford had begun producing his Model T in 1908. On May 27, 1927, the fifteen-millionth Model T was produced. And in that year, the number of Model T's still registered (and therefore still presumably on the road) came to 11,325,521. But the Model T was in trouble.

By 1920, Henry Ford's success in democratizing the automobile, in building an inexpensive car that would last forever, had produced a vast secondhand car market. Dealers faced a new kind of competition, no longer from the horse but from the millions of still-usable used Fords. At the same time, the American buying public was stirred by a rising standard of living, by rising expectations (encouraged, incidentally, by Ford's $5-a-day wage which he hoped would make it possible for still more workers to buy Fords), and by a love of speed and a love of newness. They demanded something new.

But Henry Ford's spectacular success was in producing a static model. The problems of style and consumer taste had hardly occurred to him. He was a genius at production. And with the help of his own brilliant staff, aided by the pioneer factory designer Albert Kahn and others, he had developed the assembly line and so had taken a giant step forward in elaborating the mass production which Eli Whitney had pioneered a century before.

Ironically, his faith in the Model T was an Old World faith. His belief in the perfectible product rather than the novel product, his insistence on craftsmanship and function rather than on consumer appeal eventually left him behind. His genius had heralded a new age beyond his imaginings —and not at all to his taste.

This spirit of the new age was expressed in what Charles K. Kettering and Allan Orth in 1932 called "the new necessity." "We cannot reasonably expect to continue to make the same thing over and over," they predicted. "The simplest way to assure safe production is to keep changing the product—the market for new things is infinitely elastic. . . . One of the fundamental purposes of research is to foster a healthy dissatisfaction." The leader toward the new ideal was Alfred P. Sloan, Jr., who shifted the point of view from the maker to the buyer. After Sloan went to General Motors, he developed a new and characteristically American institution. It is so familiar now that we hardly think of it as an institution. This was the annual model.

The spirit and purpose of the annual model were, of course, quite the opposite of those of Ford and his Model T. "The great problem of the future," Sloan wrote to Lawrence P. Fisher (of Fisher Body) on September 9, 1927, "is to have our cars different from each other and different from year to year." The annual model, then, was part of a purposeful, planned program. And it was based on creating expectations of marvelous, if usually vague, novelties-always-to-come.

Sloan and his able collaborators at General Motors set up a special new styling department, which soon employed over fourteen hundred people. General Motors showed a new concern for color, and even invented enticing, aphrodisiac names for old colors. Now for the first time the automobile designers included women. "It is not too much to say," Sloan explained, "that the 'laws' of the Paris dressmakers have come to be a factor in the automobile industry—and woe to the company which ignores them."

The invention of the annual model did, of course, create a host of new problems of planning and of production. How much novelty would the consumer tolerate? How to titillate and attract the buyer without frightening him by too much novelty too soon? The bulgy Buick of 1929 (nicknamed "the pregnant Buick"), which was an admirably functioning car but a disaster on the market, was, according to Sloan, the result of a design mistake of not over 1¾ inches in excess body curve.

. . .

The effort to democratize the automobile proved self-defeating—and illustrated the problem of self-liquidating ideals—in at least two other ways.

The ladder of consumption. When the Model T became cheap and reliable and almost universal, cheapness and reliability were no longer enough. To keep the automobile industry and General Motors flourishing, Sloan then devised what I would call a "ladder of consumption."

When Alfred P. Sloan, Jr., went to General Motors, the company was manufacturing numerous makes of cars. The makes had confused and overlapping markets. Sloan aimed to clarify the appeal of each General Motors make so that, for example, the Buick would plainly be a more desired car than a Chevrolet. He aimed to design a car for every purse, and to create a clear price gap between different makes. The gap, however, was not to be so great that many Chevrolet owners might not hope someday to be in the Buick class, or so that many Buick owners might not hope someday to be in the Cadillac class.

This ladder of consumption began to dominate production plans. Starting with a price schedule, Sloan then had automobiles designed to fit the prices. This required a vast and unprecedented feat of coordination. Sloan aimed at what he called the "mass-class" market. And Sloan's annual model (with the accompanying ladder of consumption) came closer than any earlier American institution to creating a visible and universal scheme of class distinction in the democratic United States of America.

The attenuation of novelty. By the late twentieth century the newness of new models had begun to consist in dubious minutiae such as concealed windshield wipers and multiple taillights. To devise every year an automobile (or rather a line of automobiles) so spectacularly different from their annual predecessors that buyers would rush to the latest model—this taxed the ingenuity of style-conscious designers and imaginative production engineers. They wracked their brains. They ran the gamut of human and diabolical ingenuity. As a result, some Chevrolets looked more impressive than some Cadillacs. The economy luxury car and the luxurious economy car were beginning to be confused. The few manufacturers—mostly foreign makers like Volkswagen and Mercedes-Benz—who did not visibly change their annual product found that they had a new sales appeal.

We cannot help recalling Henry Ford's plaint: "Change is not always progress. . . . A fever of newness has been everywhere confused with the spirit of progress." Ford himself had not imagined that the frenetic quest for annual novelty might make novelty itself pall. The success of the static model (the Model T) had itself created a demand for an annual model. The annual model ideal was itself being dissolved by success. What next?

All these are only parables of a peculiarly interesting feature of the relation of our American society to what sociologists call our values. (I prefer the commoner word, "ideals.") Anyone can think of many other comparable stories. For example, we pursue the ideal of universalizing the opportunity to travel (which makes all places more alike, and hence less worth the trouble of going to), or the ideal of indefinitely increasing leisure (which leads people to try to keep life interesting by making leisure into work), or the ideal of indefinitely increasing the means and improving the modes of communication (which leads people to communicate more and more of what is not worth communicating).

Perhaps the explanation for self-liquidating ideals is inherent in the idea of increase (which inevitably becomes excess), which has been so popular here. Perhaps it is even inherent in the ideal of democracy itself, which aims at the very same time to fulfill each unique individual and to abolish distinctions among individuals. Perhaps it is only another example of the universal tendency of love to destroy its object.

But whatever the deeper, cosmic causes, the phenomenon is, I think, obvious enough. The fact of self-liquidating ideals may help us understand some of the peculiar recurrent strains, and some of the peculiar challenges, of life in the United States today.

Old World cultures have tended to be *cumulative*—and to think of themselves as cumulative. Aristocratic cultures tended to appeal to ancient orthodoxies. To believe in the glories of France is to believe in the possibility of adding up all the disparate, conflicting achievements of different epochs of French history. Their glory is to widen the spectrum of their achievements. This requires the adding up of opposites—adding the achievements of a revolutionary republic to those of an *ancien régime*.

Old World revolutions have tended to produce explicit orthodoxies which aim to define the Good Society for all time to come.

But, starting in a new world, as a new nation, we remain a *renovating* culture. The federal experimental ideal was to make it possible to try new objectives. One of the most remarkable, and least heralded, features of our Constitution was its explicit provision for amendments.

Our recurrent need for renewal gives us some peculiarly American headaches and opportunities. For in our history there seem to be natural cycles of self-flagellation. Perhaps such recurring cycles do not come from the total failure which the self-flagellants insist upon. Perhaps they mark another age when ideals which have been substantially achieved have begun to be liquidated.

Perhaps we are witnessing an age of the self-liquidation of the ideal of the American democracy of things. Perhaps more and more Americans, surfeited by objects, many of which actually remove the pungency of experience, now begin to see the ideal—the ideal of everybody having the newest things—being liquidated before their very eyes. Perhaps the annual model has begun to lose its charm. People who are so frequently and so insistently reminded of the supposedly desirable differences between indistinguishable products, who hear the blaring of trumpets to herald a revolutionary new cold-water detergent—these people begin to be cynical about all novelty.

When the getting of more and more comes to mean less and less, when more and more Americans begin to worry about the comparative merits of their increasingly elaborate automatic appliances performing ever-more-trivial functions, is it any wonder that more and more Americans become skeptical of the salvation that lies in wealth? Is it any wonder that more Americans should begin to rediscover the basic uses of American wealth at the lowest levels of consumption? Who can doubt the satisfaction of having things or giving things when they relieve starvation or undernourishment? The poverty-Americans (who in recent years have been given the new dignity of a recognized "minority group") are perhaps the only Americans for whom the American consumption ideal has not been self-liquidating. They have not participated in either its benefits or its frustrations. Is it surprising, then, that Americans nowadays show so striking and sometimes even so militant a concern for poverty in America?

A second characteristic and growing concern of our age is the focus on environment. The word has suddenly become so popular that people act as if the very concept of environment were a creature of the mid-twentieth century, as if there had been no "environment" before. May not our new concern for the environment perhaps be another symptom of our discovery that the ideal of everything for everybody is somehow self-liquidating? By concern for environment these days we mean, of course, a concern over pollution of water and air, over congestion and crime and urban disorder—in other words for the unpredicted and uncalculated costs of building a democracy of things. So we concern ourselves less with the exhilarating prospect of making more things for everybody than with an effort (in President Nixon's phrase) to "restore nature." And we aim to cancel out some of the consequences of making so many things for everybody.

In the perspective of our history it is not surprising that we should find ourselves seeking to redefine ideals for the American nation. Perhaps it would be more comfortable to live in an age when the dominant purposes were in full flood, when the hope for fulfillment had not been overshadowed by the frustrations of fulfillment.

But may not much of the peculiar greatness of our nation consist in its uncanny and versatile powers of renewal? Again and again our nation has shown an astonishing capacity for setting itself hitherto-unimagined ideals, and then proving that these ideals can be fulfilled. And then setting still others. The burden and the challenge of being an American consist in these recurrent tests of our power of renewal. Paradoxically, this is our most distinctive and most potent tradition.

X

TECHNOLOGY AND DEMOCRACY: GETTING THERE IS ALL THE FUN

☆ ☆

One of the most interesting and characteristic features of democracy is, of course, the difficulty of defining it. And this difficulty has been compounded in the United States, where we have been giving new meanings to almost everything. It is, therefore, especially easy for anyone to say that democracy in America has failed.

"Democracy," according to political scientists, usually describes a form of government by the people, either directly or through their elected representatives. But I prefer to describe a democratic society as one which is governed by a spirit of equality and dominated by the desire to equalize, to give everything to everybody. In the United States the characteristic wealth and skills and know-how and optimism of our country have dominated this quest.

My first and overshadowing proposition is that our problems arise not so much from our failures as from our successes. Of course no success is complete; only death is final. But we have probably come closer to attaining our professed objectives than any other society of comparable size and extent, and it is from this that our peculiarly American problems arise.

The use of technology to democratize our daily life has given a quite new shape to our hopes. In this final chapter I will explore some of the consequences of democracy, not for government but for experience. What are the consequences for everybody every day of this effort to democratize life in America? And especially the consequences of our fantastic success in industry and technology and in invention?

There have been at least four of these consequences. I begin with what I call *attenuation,* which means the thinning out or the flattening of experience. We might call this the democratizing of experience. It might otherwise be described as the decline of poignancy. One of the consequences of our success in technology, of our wealth, of our energy and our imagination, has been the removal of distinctions, not just between people but between everything and everything else, between every place and every other place, between every time and every other time. For example, television removes the distinction between being here and being there. And the same kind of process, of thinning out, of removing distinctions, has appeared in one area after another of our lives.

For instance, in the seasons. One of the great unheralded

achievements of American civilization was the rise of transportation and refrigeration, the development of techniques of canning and preserving meat, vegetables, and fruits in such a way that it became possible to enjoy strawberries in winter, to enjoy fresh meat at seasons when the meat was not slaughtered, to thin out the difference between the diet of winter and the diet of summer. There are many unsung heroic stories in this effort.

One of them, for example, was the saga of Gustavus Swift in Chicago. In order to make fresh meat available at a relatively low price to people all over the country, it was necessary to be able to transport it from the West, where the cattle were raised, to the Eastern markets and the cities where population was concentrated. Gustavus Swift found the railroad companies unwilling to manufacture refrigerator cars. They were afraid that, if refrigeration was developed, the cattle would be butchered in the West and then transported in a more concentrated form than when the cattle had to be carried live. The obvious consequence, they believed, would be to reduce the amount of freight. So they refused to develop the refrigerator car. Gustavus Swift went ahead and developed it, only to find that he had more cars than he had use for. The price of fresh meat went down in the Eastern cities, and Gustavus Swift had refrigerator cars on his hands. He then sent agents to the South and to other parts of the country, and tried to encourage people to raise produce which had to be carried in refrigerator cars. One of the consequences of this was the development of certain strains of fruit and vegetables, especially of fruit, which would travel well. And Georgia became famous for the peaches which were grown partly as a result of Swift's efforts to encourage people to raise something that he could carry in his refrigerator cars.

There were other elements in this story which we may easily forget—for example, how central heating and air conditioning have affected our attitude toward the seasons, toward one time of year or another. Nowadays visitors from abroad note that wherever they are in our country, it is not unusual to find that in winter it is often too warm indoors, and in summer, often too cool.

But the development of central heating during the latter part of the nineteenth century had other, less obvious consequences. For example, as people built high-rise apartments in the cities they found it impossible to have a fireplace in every room. You could not construct a high building with hundreds of apartments and have enough room for all the chimneys. So central heating was developed and this became a characteristic of city life. As central heating was developed it was necessary to have a place to put the machinery, and the machinery went in the cellar. But formerly people, even in the cities, had used their cellars to store fruit and vegetables over the winter. When the basement was heated by a furnace, of course it was no longer possible to store potatoes or other vegetables or fruit there. This increased the market for fresh fruits and vegetables that were brought in from truck farms just outside the cities or by refrigerator cars from greater distances. And this was another way of accelerating the tendency toward equalizing the seasons and equalizing the diet of people all over the country.

Also important in attenuating experience was the development of what I would call homogenized space, especially the development of vertical space as a place to live in. There is a great deal less difference between living on the thirty-fifth floor and living on the fortieth floor of an apartment building than there is between living in a house in the middle of a block and living on the corner. The view is pretty much the same as you go up in the air. Vertical space is much more homogenized, and as we live in vertical space more and more, we live in places where "where we are" makes much less difference than it used to.

An important element in this which has been a product of American technology is, of course, glass. We forget that the innovations in the production of glass resulting in large sheets which you could look through was an achievement largely of American technology in the nineteenth century. Of course, one by-product was the development of the technology of bottling, which is related to some of the levelings-out of the seasons which I mentioned before in relation to food. But we forget that when we admire those old leaded-glass windows which we see in medieval or early modern buildings, what we are admiring is the inability of people to produce plate glass.

When a large plate of glass became technologically possible, this affected daily life in the United States. It affected merchandising, for example, because the "show window" became possible in which you could, with a relatively unobstructed view, display garments and other large objects in a way to make them appealing to people who passed by. But glass was also important in producing one of the main characteristics of modern American architecture—an architecture in which there is relatively less difference between the indoors and the outdoors than elsewhere. And that is one of the great functions of glass in modern architecture.

. . .

Along with the attenuation of places and time comes the attenuation of occasions and events. One of the more neglected aspects of modern technology is what I have called the rise of "repeatable experience." It used to be thought that one of the characteristics of life, one of the things that distinguished being alive from being dead, was the uniqueness of the individual moment. Something happened which could never happen again. If you missed it then, you were out of luck. But the growth of popular photography, which we can trace from about 1888 when Kodak #1 went on the market, began to allow everybody to make his own experience repeatable. If you had not seen this baby when he was so cute, you could still see him that way right now if you were so unlucky as to be in the living room with the parents who wanted to show you. Kodak #1 was a great achievement and was the beginning of our taking for granted that there was such a thing as a repeatable experience.

The phonograph, of course, beginning about 1877, created new opportunities to repeat audible experience. If you want to hear the voice of Franklin Delano Roosevelt now, you can hear him on a record. At the opening of the Woodrow Wilson Center for International Scholars at the Smithsonian Institution in 1971, part of the dedicating ceremony was the playing of a record with the voice of Woodrow Wilson. It was not a very warm voice, but it was identifiable and distinctive. The growth of the phonograph, then, has accustomed us to the fact that experience is not a one-time thing.

When we watch the Winter Olympics in our living room and see the ski jumper in the seventy-meter jump who makes a mistake or who performs very well, we can see the same performance just a minute later with all the failures and successes pointed out. Is instant replay the last stage in the technology of repeatable experience?

In the attenuating of events there is another element which I call the "pseudo-event." As more and more of the events which have public notice are planned in advance, as the accounts of them are made available before they happen, then it becomes the responsibility of the event to live up to its reputation. In this way the spontaneity of experience, the unpredictableness of experience, dissolves and disappears. The difference between the present and the future becomes less and less.

Another aspect of this is what I have called the "neutralization of risks," a result of the rise of insurance. For insurance, too, is a way of reducing the difference between the future and the present. You reduce risks by assuring yourself that if your house burns down, at least you will have the money so you can rebuild it. In this sense, insurance, and especially casualty insurance, provides a way of thinning out the difference between present and future, removing the suspense and the risk of experience.

What have been the everyday consequences of the democratizing of property for our experience of property? In his classic defense of property in his essay *On Civil Government* (1690), John Locke argued that because property is the product of the mixing of a person's labor with an object, no government has the right to take it without his consent. This simplistic conception of property has dominated a great deal of political and economic thinking. It was prominent in the thinking of the authors of the Declaration of Independence and of the Founding Fathers of the Constitution. It was based on a simpler society where there was something poignant and characteristic about the experience of ownership. Owning meant the right to exclude people. You had the pleasure of possession.

But what has happened to property in our society? Of course, the most important new form of property in modern American life is corporate property: shares of stock in a corporation. And the diffusion of the ownership of shares is one of the most prominent features of American life. There are companies like AT&T, for example, which have as many as a million stockholders. What does it mean to be a stockholder? You are a lucky person. You own property and you have some shares. So what? One doesn't need to be rich or even middle-class in this country to own shares of stock. But very few of my friends who own shares of stock know precisely what it means or what their legal powers are as stockholders. They are solicited to send in their proxies—by somebody who has a special interest in getting them to vote for something or other. They feel very little pleasure of control; they don't have the sense of wreaking themselves on any object. Yet this—a share of stock—is the characteristic and most important form of property in modern times. This property, too, is attenuated.

Other developments in American life concerning property have had a similar effect. For example, installment and credit buying. This phenomenon first grew in connection with the wide marketing of the sewing machine and then in relation to the cash register, but its efflorescence has come with the automobile. When it became necessary to sell millions of automobiles—and necessary in order to keep the machinery of our society going to sell them to people who could not afford to lay out the full cost of an automobile—it was necessary to find ways of financing their purchases. Installment and credit buying was developed. One of the results was that people became increasingly puzzled over whether they did or did not (and if so in what sense) own their automobile. Of course, it is not uncommon for people to divest themselves of their physical control of an object like an automobile or a color television set before they have really acquired full ownership—and then to enter on another ambiguous venture of part ownership.

Another aspect of this is the rise of franchising: the development of what I would call the "semi-independent businessman." In the United States today, between 35 percent and 50 percent of all retail merchandising is done through franchised outlets. Well, of course, we all know what a franchised outlet is; a typical example would be a McDonald's hamburger stand or any other outlet in which the person who is in control of the shop has been authorized to use a nationally advertised name like Midas Mufflers or Colonel Sanders' Kentucky Fried Chicken. He is then instructed in the conduct of his business. He must meet certain standards in order to be allowed to continue to advertise as a Holiday Inn or Howard Johnson or whatever. And he is in business "for himself." Now, what does that mean? If you go into a franchised outlet and you find the hamburger unsatisfactory, what can you do? Whom would you complain to? The man who runs the shop has received his instructions and his materials from the people who have franchised him. It is not his fault. And, of course, it's not the fault of the people at the center who franchised him, because the shop is probably badly run by the franchisee.

This phenomenon grew out of the needs of the automobile because in order to sell Fords or any other makes, it was necessary to have an outlet which would take continuous responsibility for stocking parts. Then the purchaser could replace that part at the outlet where he had purchased the car. After automobile franchising came the franchising of filling stations. People wanted some assurance about the quality of the fuel they put in their cars; they were given this by the identification of what they purchased with some nationally advertised brand in which they had confidence.

Now, perhaps the most important example of attenuation, of the decline of poignancy in our experience in relation to property, is so obvious and so universal that it has hardly been discussed. That is packaging. Until relatively recently if you went into a store to buy coffee, you would have to bring a container to the grocery store, and the grocer would ladle out the coffee to you.

Packaging began to develop in this country after the Civil War. In a sense it was a by-product of the Civil War because the necessities of the war (especially the need to package flour) produced certain innovations which were important. And later there were decisive, although what seem to us rather trivial, innovations. For example, the invention of the folding box was important. Until there was a way to make boxes which could be transported and stored compactly, it was impossible or impractical to use them for industrial purposes. The folding box and certain improvements in the paper bag, such as the paper bag that had a square bottom so that it could stand up, and on the side of which you could print an advertisement—these were American inventions.

If we will risk seeming pompous or pedantic, we can say that the most important consequences of packaging have been epistemological. They have had to do with the nature of knowledge and they have especially had the effect of confusing us about what knowledge is, and what's real, about what's form and what's substance. When you think about a Winston cigarette, you don't think about the tobacco inside the cigarette. You think about the package. And in one area after another of American life, the form and the content become confused, and the form becomes that which dominates our consciousness. One area perhaps in which this has ceased to be true, happily or otherwise, is the area which I have always thought of as an aspect of packaging—namely, clothing. In the United States we have developed ready-made clothing, too, in such a way as to obscure the differences of social class and even of sex.

All around us we see attenuation—as our technology has succeeded, as we have tried to make everything available to everybody. The very techniques we use in preparing our food, in transporting our food, in controlling the climate and temperature of the rooms we live in, the shapes of the buildings in which we do business and reside, the ways we look at past experience—in all these ways our experience becomes attenuated. As we democratize experience, the poignancy of the moment, of the season, of the control of the object, of the spontaneous event, declines.

Now to a second consequence of the success of our technology for our daily experience. This is what I would call the *decline of congregation*. Or it might be called a new segregation. This is the consequence of increasingly organized and centralized sources of anything and everything. Example: Rebecca at the well. When I wrote an article for the issue of *Life* magazine which was intended to celebrate the twenty-fifth anniversary of the introduction of television in this country, I entitled the article at first "Rebecca at the TV Set." But my friends at *Life* said, "Rebecca who?" Deferring to their greater, wider knowledge of American life and of the literariness of the American people, instead we called it simply "The New Segregation."

When Rebecca lived in her village and needed to get water for the household, she went to the well. At the well she met the other women of the village; she heard the gossip; she met her fiancé there, as a matter of fact. And then what happened? With the progress of democracy and technology, running water was introduced; and Rebecca stayed in the kitchenette of her eighth-floor apartment. She turned the faucet on and got the water out of the faucet; she didn't have to go to the well any more. She had only the telephone to help her collect gossip and she would have to find other ways to meet her fiancé. This is a parable of the problem of centralizing sources of everything.

The growth of centralized plumbing was itself, of course, a necessary by-product of the development of the skyscraper and the concentration of population in high buildings. You had to have effective sanitary facilities. But we forget other features of this development. Even those of us who have never made much use of the old "privy" know that the privy characteristically had more than one hole in it. Why was this? The plural facility was not peculiar simply to the privy; it was also found in the sanitary arrangements of many older buildings, including some of the grandest remaining medieval structures. The development of centralized plumbing led to privatizing; "privy" was the wrong word for the old facility. The privatizing of the bodily functions made them less sociable. People engaged in them in private.

The most dramatic example today of the privatizing of experience by centralizing a facility is, of course, television. We could start with the newspaper, for that matter. The town crier communicated the news to people in their presence. If you wanted to hear it you had to be there, or talk to somebody else who was there when he brought the news. But as the newspaper developed, with inexpensive printing, the messages were brought to you and you could look at them privately as you sat by yourself at breakfast. Television is perhaps one of the most extreme examples of the decline of congregation. Until the development of television, if you wanted to see a play you had to go out to a theater; if you wanted to hear a concert you had to go to a concert hall. These performances were relatively rare. They were special events. But with the coming of television, everybody acquired his private theater. Rebecca had her theater in her kitchen. She no longer needed to go out for entertainment.

The centralized source, the centralizing of the source, then, led to the isolating of the consumer. Of course, much was gained by this. But one of the prices paid was the decline of congregation—congregation being the drawing together of people where they could enjoy and react to and respond to the reactions and feelings of their fellows.

. . .

There is a third consequence of our technological success in democratic America, which I would call the new determinism, or *the rising sense of momentum.* Technology has had a deep and pervasive effect on our attitude toward history, and especially on the citizen's attitude toward his control over the future. In the seventeenth century the Puritans spoke about Providence; that was their characteristic way of describing the kind of control that God exercised over futurity. In the nineteenth century, when people became more scientifically minded, they still retained some notion of divine foresight in the form of the concept of destiny or mission or purpose. But in our time in this country we have developed a different kind of approach toward futurity; and this is what I would call the sense of momentum.

Momentum in physics is the product of a body's mass and its linear velocity. Increasing scale and speed of operation increase the momentum. One of the characteristics of our technology and especially of our most spectacular successes has been to increase this sense of momentum. I will mention three obvious examples. It happens that each of these developments came, too, as a result of overwhelming international pressure. When such pressures added to the forces at work inside the nation, in each case they produced a phenomenon of great mass and velocity which became very difficult to stop.

The first example is, of course, atomic research. The large-scale concerted efforts in this country to build an atomic bomb began and were accelerated at the time of World War II because of rumors that the Nazis were about to succeed in nuclear fission. When this information became available, national resources were massed and organized in an unprecedented fashion; futurity was scheduled and groups were set to work in all parts of the continent exploring different possible ways of finding the right form of uranium or of some other element. And the search for the first atomic chain reaction, which was accomplished at my University of Chicago, went on.

One of the more touching human aspects of this story is the account, now well chronicled by several historians, of the frantic efforts of the atomic scientists, the people who had been most instrumental in getting this process started (Albert Einstein, Leo Szilard, and James Franck, among others), when they saw that the atomic bomb was about to become possible, to persuade the President of the United States either not to use the bomb or to use it only in a demonstration in the uninhabited mid-Pacific. Such a use, they urged, would so impress the enemy with the horrors of the bomb that he would surrender, eliminating the need for us to use the bomb against a live target. They pursued this purpose—trying to put the brakes on military use of the bomb—with a desperation that even exceeded the energy they had shown in developing the bomb. But, of course, they had no success.

They could develop the bomb, but they couldn't stop it. Why? There were many reasons, including President Truman's reasonable belief that use of the bomb could in the long run save the hundreds of thousands of Japanese and American lives that would have been lost in an invasion, and also would shorten the war. But surely one reason was that there had already been too much investment in the bomb. Billions of dollars had gone into the making of it. People were organized all over the country in various ways. It was impossible to stop.

Another example of this kind of momentum is the phenomenon of space exploration. I happen to be an enthusiast for space exploration, so by describing this momentum I do not mean to suggest that I think the space enterprise itself has not been a good thing. Nevertheless, as a historian I am increasingly impressed by the pervasive phenomenon of momentum in our time. Billions of dollars have been spent in developing the machinery for going off to the moon or going then to Mars or elsewhere. The mass of the operation has been enormous. The velocity of it is enormous, and it becomes virtually impossible to stop. The recent problem with the SST is a good example. For when any enterprise in our society has reached a certain scale, the consequences in unemployment and in dislocation of the economy are such that it becomes every year more difficult to cease doing what we are already doing.

A third example, more in the area of institutions, is foreign aid: the international pressures to give foreign aid to one country or another. We have an enormous mass of wealth being invested, a great velocity with lots of people going off all over the world and performing this operation of giving aid, and it becomes almost impossible to stop it. The other countries resent the decline of aid and consider it a hostile act, even though they might not have felt that way if we hadn't started the aid in the first place. Foreign aid is, I think, the most characteristic innovation in foreign policy in this century.

Each of these three enterprises illustrates the attitude of

the American citizen in the later twentieth century toward his control over experience. Increasingly, the citizen comes to feel that events are moving, and moving so fast with such velocity and in such mass that he has very little control. The sense of momentum itself becomes possible only because of our success in achieving these large purposes which no other democratic society, no other society before us, had even imagined.

Now, what does this bring us to? Before I come to my fourth and concluding point on the ways in which the successes of democracy have affected our experience, I would like briefly to recall some of the remedies that have been suggested for the ills of democracy and the problems of democracy in the past. Al Smith once said, "All the ills of democracy can be cured by more democracy." I must confess, though I admire Al Smith for some of his enterprises, the Empire State Building for example, I think he was on the wrong track here. In fact, I would take an almost contrary position. Even at the risk of seeming flip, I might sum up the democratic paradoxes that I have been describing: "Getting there is *all* the fun."

Is there a law of democratic impoverishment? Is it possible that while *democratizing* enriches experience, *democracy* dilutes experience?

Example: photography. Before the invention of photography, it was a remarkable experience to see an exact likeness of the Sphinx or of Notre Dame or of some exotic animal or to see a portrait of an ancestor. Then, as photography was publicized in the 1880's and thoroughly popularized in this century, it opened up a fantastic new range of experience for everybody. Suddenly people were able to see things they had never been able to see before. And then what happened? Everyone had a camera, or two or three cameras; and everywhere he went he took pictures and when he came home he had to find a victim, somebody to show the pictures to. And this became more and more difficult.

While photography was being introduced, it was life-enriching and vista-opening; but once it was achieved, once everybody had a camera, the people were looking in their cameras instead of looking at the sight they had gone to see. It had an attenuating effect. A picture came to mean less and less, simply because people saw pictures everywhere. And the experience of being there also somehow meant less because the main thing people saw everywhere was the inside of their viewfinders, and their concern over their lens cap and finding the proper exposure made it hard for them to notice what was going on around them at the moment.

Another example is, of course, the phonograph. Has the phonograph—in its universal late-twentieth-century uses—necessarily made people more appreciative of music? In the 1920's when I was raised in Tulsa, Oklahoma, I had never heard an opera, nor had I really heard any classical music properly performed by an orchestra. But in our living room we had a wind-up Victrola, and I heard Galli-Curci singing arias from *Rigoletto*, and I heard Caruso, and I heard some symphonies, and it was fantastic. And then hi-fi came and everybody had a phonograph, a hi-fi machine or a little transistor radio which you could carry with you and hear music any time.

Today when I walk into the elevator in an office building,

it is not impossible that I will hear Beethoven or Verdi. Sitting in the airplane I hear Mozart coming out of the public-address system. Wherever we go we hear music whether we want to hear it or not, whether we are in the mood for it or not. It becomes an everywhere, all-the-time thing. The experience is attenuated.

And one of the most serious consequences of all this, finally, is the attenuation of community itself. What holds people together? What has held people together in the past? For the most part it has been their sense of humanity, their pleasure in the presence of one another, their feeling for another person's expression, the sound of a voice, the look on his or her face. But the kind of community I describe increasingly becomes attenuated. People are trying to enjoy the community all by themselves.

We are led to certain desperate quests in American life. These, the by-products of our success, are clues to the vitality and energy of our country, to the quest for novelty to keep life interesting and vistas open, to the quest for community and the quest for autonomy. Can we inoculate ourselves against these perils of our technological success? Samuel Butler once said, "If I die prematurely, at any rate I shall be saved from being bored by my own success." Our problem, too, is partly that.

And now a fourth characteristic of the relation of technology to democracy in our time: *the belief in solutions.* One of the most dangerous popular fallacies—nourished by American history and by some of our most eloquent and voluble patriots—is the notion that democracy is attainable. There is a subtle difference between American democratic society and many earlier societies in the extent to which their ideals could be attained. The objectives of other societies have for the most part been definable and attainable. Aristocracy and monarchy do present attainable ideals. Even totalitarianism presents objectives which can be attained in the sense in which the objectives of democracy never can be.

This nation has been a place of renewal, of new beginnings for nations and for man. Vagueness has been a national resource: the vagueness of the continent, the mystery of our resources, the vagueness of our social classes, the misty miasma of our hopes.

Our society has been most distinctively a way of reaching for rather than of finding. American democracy, properly speaking, has been a process and not a product, a quest and not a discovery. But a great danger which has been nourished by our success in technology has been the belief in solutions. For technological problems there *are* solutions. It is possible to set yourself the task of developing an economic and workable internal-combustion engine, a prefabricated house, or a way of reaching the moon. Technological problems are capable of solutions.

We are inclined, then, using the technological problem as our prototype, to believe that somehow democracy itself is a solution, a dissolving of the human condition. But we should have learned, and even the history of technology—especially the history of technology in our democratic society—should have taught us otherwise.

In human history in the long run there are no solutions, only problems. This is what I have suggested in my description of "self-liquidating" ideals. And the examples are all around us—in our effort to create a pluralistic society by assimilating and Americanizing people, in our effort to give everybody an uncrowded wilderness vacation, in our effort to find an exciting new model each year.

Every seeming solution is a new problem. When you democratize the speedy automobile and give everybody an automobile, the result is a traffic jam; and this is the sense in which the "solution" of technological problems presents us with obstacles to the fulfillment of what is human in our society. When we think about American democratic society, then, we must learn not to think about a condition, but about a process; not about democracy, but about the quest for democracy, which we might call "democratizing."

The most distinctive feature of our system is not a system, but a quest, not a neat arrangement of men and institutions, but a flux. What other society has ever committed itself to so tantalizing, so fulfilling, so frustrating a community enterprise?

To prepare ourselves for this view of American democracy there are two sides to our personal need. One is on the side of prudence and wisdom; the other on the side of poetry and imagination.

On the side of prudence, there is a need for a sense of history. Only by realizing the boundaries that we have been given can we discover how to reach beyond them. Only so can we have the wisdom not to mistake passing fads for great movements, not to mistake the fanaticisms of a few for the deep beliefs of the many, not to mistake fashion for revolution. This wisdom is necessary if we are to secure sensibly the benefits of a free society for those who have for whatever reason been deprived of its benefits. We were not born yesterday, nor was the nation. And between the day before yesterday and yesterday, crucial events have happened. We can discover these and come to terms with them only through history. As Pascal said, "It is only by knowing our condition that we can transcend it." Our technology brings us the omnipresent present. It dulls our sense of history, and if we are not careful it can destroy it.

We in the U.S.A. are always living in an age of transition. Yet we have tended to believe that our present is always the climax of history, even though American history shows that the climax is always in the future. By keeping suspense alive, we can prepare ourselves for the shocks of change.

And finally, on the side of poetry and imagination, how do we keep alive the spirit of adventure, what I would call the exploring spirit? This should be the easiest because it is the most traditional of our achievements and efforts. We must remember that we live in a new world. We must keep alive the exploring spirit. We must not sacrifice the infinite promise of the unknown, of man's unfulfilled possibilities in the universe's untouched mysteries, for the cozy satisfactions of predictable, statistical benefits. Space exploration is a symbol.

Recently I had the pleasure of talking with Thor Heyerdahl, the *Kon Tiki* man, whose latest venture was the Ra expedition, in which he explored the possibilities of men having come from Egypt or elsewhere in the Mediterranean to this continent long ago in boats made of reeds. He and his crew, to test their hypothesis, actually crossed the Atlantic in a reed boat. And as I talked to Thor Heyerdahl about the Ra expedition, I said that it must have been a terrible feeling of risk when you suddenly left the sight of land and got out into the open sea. It seemed to me that the fear and perils of the open sea would be the greatest. Thor Heyerdahl said not at all: the great dangers, the dangers of shoals and rocks, existed along the shore. The wonderful sense of relief, he observed, came when he went out on the ocean where there was openness all around, although also high waves and strong currents. The promise of American democracy, I suggest, depends on our ability to stay at sea, to work together in community while we all reach to the open horizon.

ACKNOWLEDGMENTS

The five William W. Cook Lectures which are the basis of these ten essays were delivered April 3–7, 1972, at the University of Michigan in Ann Arbor, under the general title "Frontiers of Ignorance." The individual lectures were entitled "The Idea of Negative Discovery," "Illusions of Historical Knowledge," "Prisons of History," "Temptations of the Well-Informed," and "The Omnipresent Present." I wish to thank Dean Theodore J. St. Antoine of the University of Michigan Law School, the chairman of the Cook Lecture Committee, and the other members of his committee for the privilege of participating in the fruitful tradition of that series. Also, for my wife and myself, I wish to thank the faculty of the University, and especially the faculty of the Law School and the History Department, for their warm hospitality during that stimulating week.

The essays in this book are a substantial revision of the materials of those lectures. Some of the topics had been tentatively explored even before those lectures, and others have been pursued more extensively since. I wish to thank several editors and publishers and other friends for their assistance in different versions of some of these chapters: "Overcommunication," syndicated by Field Enterprises, Inc., of Chicago, and published April 23, 1972; "Too Much Too Soon," *TV Guide,* Vol. 20 (December 16–22, 1972), pp. 14–15; "Advertising and American Civilization," a lecture at the University of Chicago (Graduate School of Business), May 24, 1973; "A Case of Hypochondria," *Newsweek* (July 6, 1970), pp. 27–29 (Copyright Newsweek, Inc. 1970. Reprinted by permission), abridged in *Reader's Digest* (September, 1970), pp. 92–94; A Statement on Quotas to the Republican Platform Committee, Miami Beach, Florida, August 16, 1972; "Democracy and the Sense of Place," a talk at the Ninth Annual Meeting of the United States Capitol Historical Society, September 15, 1971; "The Exploring Spirit," a talk at a meeting for the National Air and Space Museum, held in Washington, D.C., January 18, 1971; "Self-Liquidating Ideals," a talk to the Committee on Science and Astronautics of the U.S. House of Representatives, 91st Congress, January 28, 1970; "Technology and Democracy," a lecture at Auburn University, Auburn, Alabama, November 11, 1971, a version of which was printed in *Our Secular Cathedrals; Change and Continuity in the University* (Franklin Lectures in the

Sciences and Humanities, 3d Series; University of Alabama Press, 1973), pp. 99–123.

Since the Cook Lectures (and the others) were delivered while I was in the final stages of writing *The Americans: The Democratic Experience* (Random House, 1973), a few of the examples offered here will be found also in that volume, where some of these topics are pursued in detail. Readers who find some of these ideas provocative may wish to look at my earlier volume, *The Image: A Guide to Pseudo-Events* (1961; Atheneum paperback, 1971).

The Smithsonian Institution has continued to provide a free and encouraging scholarly environment with generous and stimulating colleagues.

I wish especially to thank Miss Genevieve Gremillion for her highly competent and always painstaking help in preparing the manuscript. Miss Alice Gergely has also helped.

My editor at Random House, Robert D. Loomis, has again given me wise counsel. Mrs. Barbara Willson has been the skillful copyeditor. Mr. Philip Lockwood has prepared the index.

This book owes more to my wife and principal editor, Ruth F. Boorstin, than to anyone else. She has given me the constant benefit of her magic feeling for words. Her collaboration has, as usual, made the making of this little book into a happy conversation.

INDEX

ABOUT THE AUTHOR

DANIEL J. BOORSTIN, senior historian of the Smithsonian Institution, Washington, D.C., was the director of The National Museum of History and Technology from 1969 to 1973. Until 1969 he was Preston and Sterling Morton Distinguished Service Professor of American History at the University of Chicago, where he taught for twenty-five years.

Dr. Boorstin has spent a good deal of his life viewing America from the outside, first in England where he was a Rhodes Scholar at Balliol College, Oxford, winning a coveted "double-first," and was admitted as a barrister-at-law of the Inner Temple, London. More recently he has been visiting professor of American History at the University of Rome and at Kyoto University, consultant to the Social Science Research Center at the University of Puerto Rico, the first incumbent of the chair of American History at the Sorbonne, and Pitt Professor of American History and Institutions and a Fellow of Trinity College, Cambridge University, which awarded him its Litt.D. degree.

Born in Georgia in 1914 and raised in Oklahoma, Dr. Boorstin received his B.A. with highest honors from Harvard and his doctor's degree from Yale. He is a member of the Massachusetts Bar and has practiced law. Before going to Chicago in 1944, he taught at Harvard and Swarthmore. He has lectured widely within this country and all over the world.

The Americans, his most extensive work, is a trilogy with a sweeping new view of American history, revealing through the story of our past some of the secrets of the distinctive character of American culture. The third volume, *The Americans: The Democratic Experience* (1973), was a main selection of the Book-of-the-Month Club. Dr. Boorstin has received several awards, including the Bancroft Prize for *The Americans: The Colonial Experience* (1958) and the Francis Parkman Prize for *The Americans: The National Experience* (1965).

Among his other books are *The Image: A Guide to Pseudo-Events in America* (1964, 1971), *The Genius of American Politics* (1953), and *The Decline of Radicalism* (1969). The editor of the 27-volume *Chicago History of American Civilization* series, he is also the author of a television show and of numerous popular articles and books.